Wiccan Spells:

A Beginner's Guide to Moon Magic, Healing, Love, and Protection Spells. Learn About the Magic Power of Elements and Learn to Use the Natural Energies of Herbs, Crystals, and Gems

Linda Buckland

Given the informational and entertainment nature of the content presented in this work, there is no guarantee as to the quality and validity of the information. As such, the contents of this work are deemed as universal. No use of copyrighted material is used in this work. Any references to other trademarks are done so under fair use and by no means represent an endorsement of such trademarks or their holder.

Table of Contents

Introduction

First off, I would like to thank you for choosing *Wiccan Spells: A Beginner's Guide to Moon Magic, Healing, Love, and Protection Spells. Learn About the Magic Power of Elements and Learn to Use the Natural Energies of Herbs, Crystals, and Gems.* I hope that you find this book informative and entertaining.

In this book, we are going to talk about three different types of magic and how you can use them in your Wiccan practice. In the first section, we are going to discuss Moon magic.

First, we will discuss what exactly Moon magic is. Since the Moon has such an influence over everything in nature, we will be discussing the power that the Moon holds over us all. This power is the reason why Wiccans will make sure their spells work at their highest power.

Then we will discuss the phases of the Moon. Each phase holds a different power, so it's important to understand their correspondences to make sure you perform the correct spells during certain phases.

Next, we will discuss special Moons. We all know the Moon isn't the same all the time. The Moon experiences eclipses, blue Moons, blood Moons, and more. Each of these special occurrences brings its own power.

The last thing we will discuss in the Moon section is how to cast circles. While casting circles doesn't directly correlate with the Moon, they are a big part in spell casting.

In the next section, we will be discussing candle magic.

First, we will discuss the power in fire, which is where the candle gets most of its power. Fire is an element that gets used a lot in magic, and candles are one of the easiest ways to bring it into your practice in a safe way.

Then we will discuss how to select your candles. There is a lot that goes into choosing a candle, such as the size, shape, and color, and understanding these things will help you to pick the best candle when the time comes.

Next, we'll discuss how to prepare your candles. Most of the time, spells will tell you how to prepare your candles; other times, they won't. Just because a spell doesn't say you have to, doesn't mean you can't. Some Witches will choose to prepare every candle they use just to make sure they get the most out of them.

The last thing you will find in this section are candle spells. As you would expect, it will be filled with spells that you can start doing with all of those candles you are sure to buy.

In the last section, we will talk about crystal magic.

First, we will discuss the power within crystals. Crystals have been used for metaphysical purposes for a very long time now, and not just in Wicca. Crystals have probably gained their popularity because of their use within meditation and Eastern cultures.

Then we will discuss the best types of crystals to use in magic. There are a lot of crystals out there, and knowing which one to choose in certain spells in important for your spells efficacy.

Next, we will go over how to pick out your crystals. Picking your crystals isn't as simple as picking one up and buying it. There is a lot that goes into it in order to make sure it is the best crystal for you.

Then we will talk about how to take care of your crystals. Crystals can be delicate creatures, so it is important that you understand the best way to take care of them so that they last the longest.

Lastly, you will find crystal spells that you can start using. They will cover many different aspects and can help improve your life in many different ways.

Let's jump right in.

Chapter 1: The Magic of the Moon

From the start of civilization, the moon has always had a very important role in the practices and myths of cultures from all over the world. For millions of years, the moon has served as a light source and a way to measure time. Just like the sun, the moon has been linked to many Goddesses and Gods in various cultures. Being used in both magic and myths, this heavenly body has been linked to many issues with our very existence like the afterlife, rebirth, death, mystery, fertility, passion, and love. The moon is still prevalent in Paganism, Witchcraft, and Wiccan practices. Normally, Wiccan covens hold rituals on the full moon so they can honor the Goddess during the Esbats. This practice can be done alone, too.

Moon's Power

Every scientist in the world knows that the Earth has an energy all its own that is different from what it gets from the Sun. The moon gives off an energy that is very distinct but subtle at the same time. Different from the sun's masculine energy, the energy from the moon is very feminine. This is the Goddess's energy. It has been described as magnetic energy that makes total sense if you have ever felt "pulled" by the moon in one way or another. People who are very sensitive can feel and actual tug in their bodies during a New or Full Moon. Other people might feel more aware of the things around them.

Lunar energy is perfect for anyone who likes tapping into their intuition. Our intuition is also called our sixth sense, and this is our most critical way of perceiving when dealing with magic. When we can consciously connect to the Moon's energy, we are literally opening a channel or path for that energy to help us make changes to our lives. If we can learn to do this on a conscious level and in harmony with the Moon's energetic rhythms, we can intensify our magic. This happens because every phase of the Moon gives us a particular energy that we can harness for certain goals.

Lunar Cycles

The relationship between the Moon and magic could be described just like the Moon as waning and waxing. While the Moon is growing, we work magic to increase, and while it is waning, we work magic to decrease. If you are looking to bring things into your life, you will work while the Moon is waxing. If you want to release or banish something you don't want in your life, you will work while the Moon is waning.

The Full Moon is the transitional point between the opposites. It is a "harvest" of sorts where we can celebrate the things we have manifested during the first part of the cycle. We will then clean up. We will find and release things that we don't need during the next part of the cycle. During the New Moon, we will set our new intentions for the next manifestation, and the cycle continues. You can visualize this rhythm as the tides rolling in and out of the sea. Here are a few suggestions to help you time your magic to the Moon's phases:

- Dark Moon: During the day right before a New Moon, most witches won't work magic. They choose to refresh their energy for the next waxing cycle. There are others who find the Dark Moon is the best time to work magic that is related to closure, and this will bring things to a full circle. The Moon's energy holds a destructive potential that you can use to release any karma that keeps popping into your life over and over again, like things related to betrayal, abandonment, or lack. Some gems you can use during this time are clear quartz, obsidian, and tektite.

- Waning Moon: This would be the time for you to release energy outwardly and align yourself with inward energy. This will get rid of all negative experiences and energies. Your main goal is to do spells that help you get rid of anything that is causing sickness, resolve conflicts, and overcome obstacles.

Some gems you can use during this time are unakite jasper, angelite, obsidian, petalite, black tourmaline, and calcite.

- Full Moon: This Moon phase is the most powerful in the whole lunar cycle. Most witches consider the day of the Full Moon the most magically powerful day during the whole month. They usually save their spell work that is related to important goals for this day. All magic is favored when done during a ritual under the Full Moon. Some gems you could use during this time are quartz, selenite, and moonstone.

- Waxing Moon: This is the perfect time to take action toward your goals. Beginning these goals during this time will bring you to them faster. This energy is action energy, and it will push your intentions out into the Universe. The magical work you do during this time should be related to strengthening or gaining partnerships with other people. It might be a business partner, romantic partner, or making new friends. It is also a time to improve your well being and physical health. Gems you can use during this time are emerald, rainbow moonstone, citrine, carnelian, and fluorite, and nuumite.

- New Moon: This is the beginning of the lunar cycle. This is the time to dream about what you want to create in life. Magic meant to begin new ventures or projects are great to do during this time. Basically, anything that involves increasing or attracting the things you desire would be great. Some gems you can use during this time are the clear quartz, obsidian, tektite, iolite, black moonstone, and labradorite.

Chapter 2: The Power of the Moon

First, let us remember that the human body is made up of 60% water. The Earth is also covered by 70% water. So, why wouldn't the Moon's energy affect us when the Moon alone is able to create high tides? We are one with the Earth. The Earth is part of us. We are the Moon, sky, and oceans. This energy is always around us, whether we pay attention to it or not. Did you know that the Moon does not actually create its own light. Instead, it is illuminated by the reflection of the light of the Sun. Yet you can see the power of the Moon, and it can be felt in many different ways.

You may already know that you enjoy sitting outside and gazing up at the Moon on a clear night. You may also find that you are mesmerized by its beauty and image how another person is sitting somewhere else is able to see the exact same thing that you are seeing.

But did you realize that this celestial body is able to affect your daily actions and choices? Most everybody has heard old farmers talking about how it is important to plant your crops according to the cycle of the Moon. And we all know how people say a Full Moon brings out all the crazy people.

If you don't believe me, all you have to do is ask a police officer or look through some hospital records. More mayhem and crime seems to happen during a Full Moon.

The thing is, it's not just crazy people who come out during the Full Moon. Babies tend to be born more often during a Full Moon. Plus, it is believed that romance will bloom on a clear night under the light of the Full Moon.

Everything living on Earth is greatly affected by the cycles of the Moon. While there are scientists who have tried to debunk this idea, there are many more anecdotes and legends that hand around about the "madness" that occurs during the Full Moon. The thing is, it's not just the Full Moon that is able to affect our actions, energy levels, and moods. Every single phase has a unique effect on us and everything in nature.

This is why it is so important that you align your energy to the energy of the Moon. You may find that during certain phases, you are naturally pulled into organizing things, evaluating your life, or taking inventory of things you have.

While the Full Moon can create chaos and craziness, the New Moon is not as showy. It is a time that is more relaxing, and you may be naturally drawn to setting intentions or seeing what you have accomplished.

Humans were more affected by the Moon during ancient times because they didn't have electricity or our modern amenities. A lot of the women would start their menstrual cycle when the Moon was in her dark phase. This is when they would retreat into their "red tent" or "moon lodge." The men were left to take care of themselves, the chores, and the children.

If modern women have the chance to take a few days off each month during their period where they didn't have to worry about their responsibilities, perimenopause and menopause wouldn't hit them so hard. Unfortunately, we no longer have Moon lodges, and bosses and families look at women as the only person who can take care of household chores.

Moods and the Moon

It has already been mentioned that on the night of the Full Moon, more things go haywire in the human world. But, if you're still not quite on board with the Moon affecting our moods, let alone when women give birth or have their menstrual cycle, I would like to present to you a real life situation.

One man was admitted to a psychiatric ward in 2005 because of violent mood swings. His mood would swing violently from one extreme to the other and would sometimes cause suicidal fantasies or hearing things that weren't actually there. His sleep pattern was also erratic and would swing from insomnia to sleeping 12+ hours each night.

His doctor kept meticulous records of his mood and sleep patterns to try to make sense of it all. The doctor found that the man's mood and sleep patterns seemed to track with the rise and fall of the oceans. Typically, if there was a high tide, the man's sleep duration would be short. This particular man was simply given pills and light therapy to control his mood, and nothing else was done about this hunch the doctor had.

12 years after that, Thomas Wehr, a renowned psychiatrist, published a paper that described 17 patients who suffered from rapid-cycling bipolar disorder. This was a form of illness marked by a person switching between mania and depression more quickly than most. They also showed an uncanny regularity in their moods, like the last person we talked about.

Since the beginning of time, humans have believed that the Moon controls our moods. We get the word lunacy from the Latin word lunaticus, which means moonstruck. Pliny the Elder, a Roman naturalist, and Aristotle, a Greek philosopher, both believed that epilepsy and madness were caused by the Moon. While studies on the Moon affecting births, criminal activity, and violence are inconclusive, there is definite evidence that the Moon affects our sleep cycle.

A 2013 study, which was highly-controlled, found that people slept 20 minutes longer and took five more minutes to fall asleep around the Full Moon, even though they were never exposed to Moonlight. Their brain activity, though, suggested that their time in deep sleep had a drop of 30%.

If you deep dive into the studies performed on humans to see how they respond to the Moon, you are going to come across the same thing, "We aren't certain that the Moon is to blame." Scientists may not be able to fully accept the fact that humans are indeed affected by the Moon; they can't ignore this phenomenon. Otherwise, they wouldn't have come up with the hypothesis that they study.

High Tides and the Moon

Now, the Moon doesn't just affect the birth of babies, crime, menstrual cycles, and organization. It also has an effect on the Earth in the form of tides. Both the Moon and the Sun influences the tides, but the Moon plays a bigger role. The Moon is much closer to the Earth than the Sun is, and the tidal effect that the Moon has is twice as strong as the Sun's.

We are going to dive into a bit of science for a moment. The Sun and Moon have a gravitational force that affects the Water in our oceans, which causes it to bulge on opposite sides of Earth. Since the Earth rotates, the two bulges act like "waves" that continuously undulate around Earth. At mid-ocean, these waves are a little under a yard high when you compare them to the water level of the troughs between them.

The acts of the tides are one of the most reliable phenomena that happen in the world, and we understand that they move in and out about twice each day, but this isn't exact. Why is that so?

Well, a single day on Earth is how long it takes Earth to spin around once on its axis in relation to the Sun. This is what is referred to as a solar day and takes 24 hours. However, for the Earth to reach the same position in relation to the Moon, it takes 24 hours and an extra 50 minutes, which is what is called a lunar day. The reason for this is that the Moon revolves around Earth in the same direction that Earth moves. This is why it takes Earth 50 minutes to catch up.

Since the Moon's tidal force is twice as strong as the Sun's, the movement of the tides follows lunar days. This means that it takes half of a lunar day, about 12 hours and 25 minutes, to go from one high tide to the next. This is why we have high and low tides about twice each day.

Animals and the Moon

In Southern California, about twice a month from March to August, people will gather on the beaches to watch a spectacle each evening. This is when grunions lunge themselves onto the shore as far as they can to mate. Their mating ritual is timed to the tides, as well as the hatchings that happen about ten days later. The larvae emerge every two weeks from the eggs, and this coincides with the peak high tides. This is because the baby grunions need the tides to wash them back out to sea.

The person choreographing this grunion mating dance and birth is none other than the Moon. Science tells us the Moon affects the tides, but it is a lot harder to imagine that the Moon also affects living creatures, especially for those who live in cities that are filled with artificial lights.

All throughout the animal kingdom, the absence or presence of Moonlight, and its predictable changes can shape many important activities. Among those things are communication, reproduction, and foraging. Research has found that Moonlight can influence the growth of fish, the navigation of dung beetles, the behavior of lion prey, as well as birdsong.

Lions in the Serengeti are considered night stalkers. The most successful ambush animals, which can include humans, happen during the darker Moon phases. But how their prey responds to the change in predator threats as the light during the night changes during the month has always been a mystery.

The lion's prey, buffalo, gazelles, zebras, and wildebeests, are plant eaters. They have to forage a lot to meet their food needs, even if that means going out at night. Some new studies have found how their foraging changes depending on the lunar cycle.

The common wildebeest tends to be the most attuned to the lunar cycle. They create their entire night based on what phase the Moon is in. At the darkest parts of the month, they would stay in areas they deemed as safe. When the nights became brighter, wildebeests were willing to venture into areas where lion might be.

Now, the African buffalo is the most daunting prey of the lion, and they are also the least likely to change how they act throughout the lunar cycle. But, when the nights were darker, they were more likely to create herds to make grazing safer.

Zebras and gazelles changed up their evening routines based on the lunar cycle. Unlike other pretty, they reacted more directly to the change in the Moon. Gazelles did more once the Moon came up. Zebras would sometimes start moving about and doing things before the Moon came up. This may seem risky, but being unpredictable could play a part in the zebra's defense.

The Moon doesn't just affect nocturnal creatures. For example, the white-browed sparrow weavers live in families. All year, they sing together in order to defend their home. But, when it's breeding season, the males will perform solos at dawn.

During the mating season on the morning after a Full Moon, the male birds would wake up ten minutes earlier to start singing than if there had been a New Moon. The extra light of the Full Moon helps to kick start their singing.

It's not that hard to look throughout nature to see things that are affected by the Moon. With all of these correlations, why wouldn't you want to make sure your magic matches up with the cycle of the Moon? Your body already does.

Chapter 3: Moon Phases

In the first chapter, I talked a little bit about the different phases of the Moon; now, we are going to look at each phase of the Moon and the things it can do for you. You will find spells and rituals that are related to each phase.

Living by the Moon helps to make your life more efficient. As a magic practitioner, when you time your rituals and spells with the phases of the Moon, it can feel like swimming with the current. It makes things go smoothly. They get an added oomph in their power as well. Working your life with the Moon's cycles can help you to feel more energetic and healthier, and it can aid in helping you give up your old habits. The key is to make sure that you work with nature.

Regardless of whether or not a person views themselves as a witch or not, the majority of humans will feel some sort of connection to the Earth's natural satellite. Witches often view the Moon as the Mother Energy, and the Sun is the Father Energy. Since the Moon controls the tides and the human body is made up of about 60 percent water, it makes sense that the phases of the Moon affect us. So how can we use the phases of the Moon in our magic?

Moon rituals are a sacred and ancient practice that has roots in Egypt, India, Babylonia, and China, where worshiping the Moon was part of their culture. They understood that the phases of the Moon influenced the decline or growth of their plants, humans, and animals. Basking up the moonlight was viewed as something sacred and needed as part of each cycle.

In today's time, the Moon ritual carries a similar sacredness and brings about a primal practice into the world. These rituals are things that we need in our lives, especially when life is full of despair, challenges, and heartbreak. The most beautiful part about rituals is that they give you a chance to be quiet. They ask you to set intentions and to connect with the environment. You will find rituals in the next sections of this chapter.

New Moon

The New Moon is everybody's fresh start. This is the time where you don't see the Moon at all, and the sky looks black, except for the stars. Magic has a tendency to be quite literal, and when the Moon isn't in the sky, this can be the best time to work on the shadow self or acknowledge your dark sides that are normally hidden away from people. This is also a good time for starting new things and new beginnings.

For example, maybe you have a bit of a manipulative streak, and you often try to ignore this part of you even if you're called out. Are there any good ways that you could use this skill, like getting ahead in your career without hurting other people? Maybe you could also use your skills to read other people so that you can encourage them to communicate more so that you don't control them. This is the time of cycle to explore your shadow side and find positive ways to use them.

Additionally, since the new moon is the beginning of the phase, it is a great time to set intentions and goals for the cycle. How would you like your next month to look? Is there a toxic person that you would like to cut ties with? The New Moon is the perfect time to encourage new beginnings, especially when they have to do with love. Guess what beginnings require... letting go of the past? If you want to let go of bad energy within your love life in order to attract your soul mate, then the New Moon can help you.

A good idea for your magic during this time is to try some bath magic. Your bathtub is basically a gigantic cauldron. Water and salt are very cleansing, so run a bath and fill it up with some bath salts or sea salt. You can even try using some witchy bath bombs if you want to. Really set the mood by lighting a few candles. Take a relaxing bath and start picturing all of your past pains and hurts being washed away by the water and then draining away as you drain out the water. Sure, you can make details and intricate spells, but they don't always have to be. They can be just simple and natural as taking a nice bath.

New Moon Ritual

To begin this ritual, you will need to organize and clean your space. This is something that you should be before every ritual. Getting rid of excess clutter and straightening up helps to set a clear intention and tone for your ritual. Burning some sage, lighting a candle, and playing some soothing music will help to clear out the energy. You should also keep a pen and paper close just in case you need it.

Next, create a connection with your Divine. This would be the time to cast a circle and call the four elements into your ritual. Then call in the Sun and Moon to represents the God and Goddess.

Once you are ready, sit inside your circle and grab that pen and paper you have and start to write down the things in your life that you either want to create or your want to get rid of. These could be barriers, feelings, or fears; basically, anything that isn't serving anymore. Consider these things that you want to bring into your life. This can be anything and everything you want, financial abundance, a relationship, a job, a new adventure, anything at all.

Now, read the things that you want to bring into your life out loud. Saying these things out loud is essential to bringing them to fruition. You may even find that they cause an emotional response when you speak them, and this feeling is extremely important for them to manifest.

Last, you just need to sit quietly and allow your desires to sit with you. Focus on your breath and visualize all of your desire coming true. Set the intention to remain open to all of the elements and experiences that are coming to life, and all other growth opportunities that you may need to have along the way.

Once you are done meditating, close your circle and thank all the deities that you called for help for being with you and guiding you.

Waxing Moon

The waxing phase of the Moon is when the Moon starts to get bigger, moving from the New Moon to the Full Moon. During this phase, the Moon is growing and turning brighter, and this is the perfect phase for growth and sympathetic magic. Sympathetic magic is the type of magic that works through symbolic resemblance. Since the Moon is growing, we need to use this energy to make you love life, self-esteem, and career brighter.

Some people like to break waxing and waning phases down into three parts. The first section of the waxing Moon is the waxing crescent. This is where the moon looks like a smile. This part continues until the first quarter with the Moon is half full. Then it becomes a waxing gibbous where the Moon looks fatter before it becomes full.

The waxing crescent period can help to bring things out. This is a great time for constructive magic. This is a great time to do magic on yourself that pertains to new beginnings, like making future plans or projects. If you want to bring new energies into your life, like patience, and a positive attitude, this is a great time for these types of goals. People who are artistic or creative love this time of the Moon's phase for spell work. This time brings more passion and inspiration to your work.

During the first quarter, the Moon's energy is connected to attraction. This is a great time for magic that draws things to you. This is a great time for meditations and spells that are meant to bring things into your life like success, protection, and money. This is also a great time to attract people like clients, lovers, and friends. If you are trying to find something that you have lost, or are trying to buy a house, this is a great time to perform spells for success with these things.

The waxing gibbous is also a great time for constructive magic, which is best oriented around "reeling in" the things that you have been working on. If you have been working on something and it has stalled, floundered, or you are coming into the home stretch, use this energy to bring it around and push it home. This time has a lot of energy for renewing your strength, determination, and will.

Some great ideas for magic during the entire waxing phase is to write out a letter of intent that states what you would like to get from your career. This could mean a raise or a change in your position, or it could be a complete change in careers. Evidence has proven that writing down things and journaling is a great emotional process and helps you to go after the things that you want. If you are looking to make more money, get a green candle, if you can't find one, a plain white one will work just as well.

To keep things different, carve your name into the candle along with different money symbols that represent your desires. Read the letter you wrote out loud with intention and meditate on it. Visualize yourself getting whatever it is that you want because you deserve it. Then you should light the candle and let it burn out. This transmits your desires out into the Universe.

Full Moon

The Full Moon can be a crazy time. Some wild things seem to happen during this phase of the Moon. Emotions are often elevated during this time, and everything tends to be intense. This intensity can be harnessed and used for pretty much any spell. A lot of people like to charge their crystals during this phase of the moon by putting them either outside or in a windowsill to be exposed to the Moon's light. You can also create a Full Moon by putting a cup of water under the light of the Full Moon. You can also place a letter if intention underneath the cup of water. Allow the water to be charged by the Moon, and then you can drink it.

You can do pretty much any type of magic under the Full Moon and gain extra power, but this is also a time where your psychic abilities are stronger. You should trust your instincts during this time, even if your emotions are running crazy. One of the easiest ways to use the Full Moon's energy is to meditate under the light of the Full Moon for clarity.

Some great magic to practice during this phase is sex magic and use the power of an orgasm to manifest what you want. Open up your shades and a window to allow the light of the

Moon to shine in. You can do sex magic by yourself or with a partner. As you orgasm, visualize your intention, whatever it may be. Sex and the Full Moon is a recipe for success.

Full Moon Ritual

Since there is a lot of energy during this time, it is a good idea to bring calmness into your area so that you will be able to harness all of the energy to benefit you. Sage your space, take a few cleansing breaths, and try to relax.

Take some time to think about the past month. What types of things have happened? What things did you succeed with? What problems did you face? Where do you think you could improve and grow?

Once you are clear on the things that you have brought into your life and what you haven't, you need to write down and release whatever it is that is getting in the way of your experiences that you haven't brought into your life. You can do this by either flushing or burning away the blocks.

If you are able to go outside and allow the Moon to touch you. The sunlight gives us Vitamin D that helps nourish our bodies, but the moonlight also benefits you. Moonlight is believed to reduce inflammation, and it can also help a woman's menstrual cycle.

Whether you are celebrating or you are trying to call in your dreams, dance around to your favorite music to get rid of stagnant energy and to bring in more joy and light.

Waning Moon

The waning period of the Moon is a time where the Moon is growing smaller, heading back to the New Moon. The waning phase is a great time for banishing work or to cut cords with people. However, banishing a person from your life completely may not have to always be done. Some of the more powerful banishing work that can be done are spells that get rid of feelings for a person that you know isn't good for you, self-doubt, or insecurity. Spells that tend to work better than banishing spells are working on changing yourself. Get rid of those thoughts that keep telling you that you don't deserve anything better because you do deserve better. Get rid of unfair treatment at your job. Get rid of unwanted negativities that are keeping you from getting the things you deserve.

Like the waxing phase, the waning phase is made up of three parts: the waning gibbous, the third quarter, and the waxing crescent. They look the same as the waxing phase, just in reverse.

Minor banishings are a great thing to do during the waning gibbous. This would be the time to clean your home, garden, office, and other personal spaces so that things don't end up building up. You can cleanse personal objects during this time too. Doing this regularly is a good idea. If you need some sort of closure, or you want to end something, this is a good time to perform spells for just that. This is a good time for introspection.

The third quarter is when you should deal with obstacles that could be standing in your way of reaching your goals. Whenever you are trying to work towards something, there will be roadblocks. This Moon phase will provide you with appropriate energies to deal with these. Temptations are something that you can deal with during this time as well. This time can also help you through transitions.

The waning crescent is a good time to clear your home and life of stress, chaos, negativity, strife, and so much more. This is a suitable time for stronger banishing spells than any other time during the waning phase. This is the time to get rid of anything that has really been concerning, annoying, or frustrating you.

Some other great spells that you may want to perform during this entire phase could include writing your insecurities and fears down. There are some people who will take these things to a crossroads to get rid of it. You don't have to do it this way, though. You can simply burn it and then bury ashes.

When it comes to aligning your spell work up with the moon phases, don't overthink it. While you may think that the closest Moon phase doesn't work for the spell you need to do, think again. You may not want to wait three weeks for the best phase, so see if there is a time to work around it. Also, this isn't an exact science. You and your intention is the most important thing in your magic practice, so focus on that and do your best and time your spells with the Moon.

Chapter 4: Special Moons

Other than the various phases of the Moon, there are other specialty Moons that can offer you more power. The main two specialty Moons that witches look for are the Blue Moon and eclipses. These times of the year are rare, especially the Blue Moon, as it offers you extra power for your magic.

Lunar Eclipses

Before we jump into the magical powers of the lunar eclipse, let's look at the science behind an eclipse.

The Moon, by itself, doesn't give off any light. The light that we are able to see is the sunlight reflecting off the surface of the Moon. A lunar eclipse happens when the Earth's shadow blocks the sunlight, which makes it look temporarily dark. Unlike with solar eclipses, which only specific areas of the world can see, a lunar eclipse can be seen by any area that is dark enough when it happens.

The shadow of the Earth is called its umbra. Specifically, the umbra is the darkest part of the shadow of the Earth. The outer edge of the shadow is called the penumbra.

There are several different types of lunar eclipses. The first is the penumbral lunar eclipse. This is where the Moon passes through the outer shadow of the Earth, which creates partial darkness of a part of the Moon. You can have a total penumbral lunar eclipse. This is where the Moon is completely shadowed b the penumbra, but it never reaches the umbra.

Then there is a partial lunar eclipse. This is where the umbra of the Earth shadows a significant portion of the Moon, but doesn't cover it completely.

Then there is a total lunar eclipse. This is where the Moon is completely covered by the umbra and fully shadowed. However, since there is light refracted through the atmosphere of the Earth, the Moon will look a bit reddish.

Then there is a selenelion. This is a horizontal eclipse, and only occurs if the sun and the Moon are visible when it happens.

Scientists like to measure the brightness of the Moon during a total lunar eclipse around mid-totality using what is called the Danjon Scale. This scale was created by the French astronomer, Andre Louis Danjon.

0 – is when the eclipse is very dark and is pretty much invisible.

1 – is when the eclipse is dark and either dark brown or grey in color.

2 – is when the eclipse is brick-red. There will be an umbral shadow that has a yellow edge.

4 – is when the eclipse is copper-red. There will be an umbral shadow with a bluish edge.

Another very specific type of lunar eclipse that witches love is called the Blood Moon. On the Danjon Scale, the Blood Moon is considered level three. The Blood Moon is when an eclipse happens when the Moon is in its closest position to the Earth, which is called perigee. Whenever the Full Moon happens at perigee, you will likely hear the phrase "Super Full Moon."

Despite the name, there isn't anything ominous about the Blood Moon. This Moon is seen as more witchy because it looks red. Within the scientific community, this color-changing phenomenon is referred to as Rayleigh Scattering.

Raleigh scattering helps to describe how the sunlight appears to change colors as it moves through the atmosphere of the Earth. The atmosphere works like a filtration system for the sunlight. While sunlight is considered to be "white" light, we know that it really contains the full visible spectrum of colors that are seen whenever light passes through a prism. This is the reason why we sometimes see rainbows whenever it rains because the water vapor acts like tiny prisms.

Having a basic understanding of this scientific wisdom is very helpful when it comes to your magic practice. It explains the mechanisms that help to fuel our work during a lunar eclipse. If we don't understand how the material world works, it is possible that we could fall prey to superstitions and fear-mongering that surrounds these natural occurrences. Witches don't allow fear to control them. Knowledge is power.

So here is a quick little science lesson for you. Depending on the sun's angle, and the amount of Earth's gasses, water vapor, and volcanic dust that is moving through the atmosphere, these things shift the wavelength of the sun's light. The colors on the red end of the spectrum will have longer wavelengths, and their frequencies are lower than the other colors. The colors on the violet end have higher frequencies and shorter wavelengths. The Rayleigh scattering effects is the reason that sunrises and sunsets look orange and red in color.

So, the Blood Moon looks red because it only has a small amount of light to reflect back onto the Earth's surface. Since red is least altered during the filtration process, you only get to see the color that was able to survive the trip. This means that the Moon reflects red back onto the Earth.

There are many legends and folklore surrounding lunar eclipses.

Christopher Columbus used his almanac to figure out that there would be a lunar eclipse in February. He used this piece of information to scare some natives of Jamaican into offering shelter and food to him and his men. He told the chieftain that God was angry with the natives didn't want to help him. He told them that God was going to turn the Moon blood red, and then take it away to show his displeasure. The Moon did disappear, and this created a lot of terror for the locals. Right before the eclipse ended, Columbus told them that God would forgive the natives as long as they made sure that the sailors were fed. The Moon came back, and Columbus and his mean got to eat very well until the next ship arrived.

In Benin, Africa, a tribe there views the lunar eclipse as a time of battle between the Moon and the sun. They dance and chant during this time to encourage their reconciliations into the sky. They used the period as a way to sort through quarrels that they are having, much like the sun and Moon resolving their feud once the eclipse ends.

In Norse mythology, a monster called Managarmr, the Moon Hound eats the Moon and stains the sky in blood during

Ragnarok. Managarmr is the son of a giantess and Fenrir, the grey wolf.

There are some practitioners who view the eclipse as being the equivalent of a full lunar cycle packed into a single event. After all, the Moon does look like it is going from waning, waxing, and reappearing during the eclipse.

There are some modern traditions that consider the eclipse as a metaphysical bonus round. Basically, any spell work that is done during this time is amplified and has extra power. So what kind of magic is best done during an eclipse? Eclipses only take place during the Full Moon, so keep your intentions turned towards spiritual development and personal growth.

Most Wiccans see the lunar energy during an eclipse to be more potent. There are several different ways to look at this energy. It could be, as mentioned earlier, that you get all of the energy from each phase in one single night, but there is another way you can look at it. You can look at the energies of the sun, Earth, and Moon in alignment. The Moon is reflecting the energy of the Earth and sun back on to the Earth. The Moon and sun will be in opposite Zodiac signs during an eclipse.

Also, if there is a lunar eclipse taking place somewhere, you can still harness its power even if you can't physically see it. It is all in your intention.

But why, exactly, do Witches care so much about all of these special lunar eclipses like the Blood Moon?

The simplest answer is that when the Moon is close to the Earth, it has a strong pull on the tides. The interaction between the sunlight, its passage through the atmosphere, and its reflection off of the Moon that is created by the eclipses moves the Moon's energy into the "red" end of the light spectrum. All of this relates to the element of Earth, the root chakra, and our animalistic survival needs.

The long explanation; when I said "tides," I was referring to more than the ocean. In Wicca, and other Pagan traditions, it is understood that the ocean is simply a metaphor for our mysteries and depths. The Moon affects how water flows, and this same power ebbs and flows through all of us with our emotions, moods, instincts, and intuitions.

Let's look at this metaphorically. The sun represents our outer persona, the conscious thoughts we make, our energy, our will, and how we project the power in the world to make the life we live. The Earth represents the body, our home, our material world, and our sustenance. The Moon represents our intuition, our subconscious mind, and our shadow illusions that can change our true will. These things are in a near perfect line where the material self is shifted, and the conscious self is changed to show and energize our deepest desires.

This is a lot of crazy cosmic drama. So when a Blood Moon occurs, take a look into the Zodiac signs to see what special conditions are being enhanced and use that information.

The way that the lunar eclipse will affect you depends on the astrological sign that the eclipse occurs in. It is important that we don't forget that the stars surrounding the Moon set the stage for all of these solar system movements. To figure out what drama the Moon will intensify, you need to look at the Zodiac.

Each Full Moon happens because the Moon is 180 degrees opposite the sun. This creates a gateway effect for everybody on the Earth, where we are in the middle of polar opposites. Knowing the spectrum that we are placed in during the eclipse helps us to work with the eclipse.

So, if the eclipse happens when the sun is in Aquarius, then the Full Moon will happen on the opposite end in Leo, which is what happened on January 20, 2019. These two signs are fixed in Air and Fire. Aquarius' dreamy thought process is empowered by the bold action of Leo that helps to support our egos.

There are 12 possible mixtures of Zodiac signs within eclipses. You will have to figure out this for each eclipse before it happens in order to use its power. Since an eclipse will put the Earthly, material spin on your conscious and subconscious dreams, it creates a very strong gateway through which you can use to bring your hidden desires to heart.

Lunar Love Spell

If the lunar eclipse falls in Leo, this spell will be more powerful.

You are going to need:

- Gold candle

- Picture of whatever you are trying to attract or something that symbolizes it

- Sage or favorite incense

- Pen

- Essential oil – choose your favorite or mix them before you cast the spell

- Paper

Start by clearing your space and altar by burning some sage or incense. Take the time to cast a circle, call on the elements, and any guides that you want to protect and help you with your spell.

Once you know exactly what you want, write it down with as many details as you can using the pen and paper that you have. You want to really feel everything that you are writing down. As you write it, make sure you visualize it, too. After everything is written down, now write: "thank you for bringing (the things you want) into my life now." Your guides and the Universe like to be recognized.

When you have finished writing, anoint your candle with your mixture of oils. Do this by pulling the oil from the bottom up the candle and out toward you. You should also anoint the picture or symbolic representation of what you want in your life.

Now, burn the paper that has your intentions written on it. Keep everything safe by burning it in a fire-proof bowl. Put the ashes of the paper and place them in a potted plant and mix it into the dirt. This will help your intentions come to life.

Each day, for one week, light a candle. Make sure the symbolic representation of your intention is kept with you whenever you light the candle, and acknowledge your guides and thank them.

Blood Moon Spell

For this spell, all you will need is a calm mind and yourself. It is a good idea to meditate before you begin.

To start, you need to take a ritual bath. Sit in the bath and visualize all of your negative energy being washed away. Then, when you drain all of the water out of the tub, believe that all of that negativity is being drained away.

When the eclipse is getting ready to happen, step outside, and find a place where you can view the Moon clearly. Once is Moon is completely eclipsed, say: "I summon the Triple Goddess in all her names, forms, and faces. I summon the Maiden, Mother, and Crone and ask them kindly to grant me a wish. I wish (state what you want and be as explicit as you can). I thank you, great Triple Goddess. As I will so mote it be. Blessed be."

Go back inside and know that your wish has been heard.

Lunar Spell for Freedom, Gratitude, and Strength

This is a great spell whenever you are finding it hard to detach yourself from things that are no longer serving you.

You are going to need:

- Musical instrument

- An altar

- A black or white candle

Begin by casting a circle and summoning the elements, God, and Goddess, and whoever else you would like to call in for this spell. Some good Goddesses to call in for this spell are Nyx, Kali, Nyphthys, and Hekate.

You don't have to go outside to do this spell, but you can if you want. It is going to feel amazing. Begin by lighting the candle. Pick up the musical instrument, even if it is something you have had to improvise. The important thing is that you feel comfortable. Allow the energy of the eclipse to guide you as you play the instrument. While you are playing, say: "In the light of the lunar eclipse, I summon thee oh (your chose guide), to stay with me. The power of the Moon, together with the sun, is providing me with strength for my journey has begun. I, (say your name), am here to honor my Goddess, my God, and my ancestors for everything they have made for me. I am free from my habits (think about old habits you want to release). I am free from my addictions (again, think about any addictions you want to release). I am free from my problems (think about the problems). Under the shadow, I begin a new path full of blessings and motivation. The sun will guide me, and the Moon will light my inspiration. I thank thee! I thank thee! I thank thee!"

Allow the candle to burn out. You can have fun at this time in whatever way you want. Once the candle is out, close your circle and thank your guides.

Magic of the Blue Moon

In today's time, a Blue Moon refers to the occasions when there are two Full Moons in a single month. The majority of the time, there is only one Full Moon is a month, but sometimes a second Full Moon can fall into a month. The only month of the year that can't have a Blue Moon is February. Some Blue Moons, according to this definition, that has happened or will happen occurred on July 31st in 2015, the first Full Moon was July 2nd; January 31st in 2018, where the first Full Moon occurred on January 2nd; March 31st of 2018, where the first Full Moon occurred in March 2nd;

and October 31st of 2020, where the first Full Moon will occur on October 1st.

The Sky & Telescope magazine, in 1946, erroneously referred to a Blue Moon as a month that has an extra Full Moon. This is the definition that caught on and is what most people believe.

Before this, a Blue Moon referred to having an extra Full Moon during any season. Season refers to a span of time between solstices and equinoxes. Most of the time, each season will have three Full Moons, but sometimes there will be a fourth. Since every Full Moon has its own name associated with its season, an extra Moon can mean that the names line up wrong, so the additional Moon gets a different name, so it is referred to as a Blue Moon. Blue Moons, in this definition, are the third Full Moon during a season that will have four Full Moons.

These Blue Moons tend to happen once every 2.7 years. Some Blue Moon dates, following this definition, are May 21, 2016, May 18, 2019, August 22, 2021, and August 19. 2024.

Blue Moons, according to the first definition, tend to happen more often than the other types of Blue Moon. When you hear somebody talk about a Blue Moon, there is a good chance they are referring to the first definition. However, this definition is dependent on an arbitrarily imposed month lengths while the second goes with the natural cycle. For most Wiccans, Pagans, astronomers, and astrologers, they follow the second definition that follows the seasons is the most useful. That being said, it tends to be harder to track, and most people will just follow the first definition.

The Blue Moon is twice as powerful as the regular Full Moon. This is a good time to perform anything that needs an extra kick. Any spells, intentions, or rituals performed during this moon are great for long-term results because it really sets things in motion and helps you to read your end result.

You can harness the magic of the Blue Moon to invoke spiritual energy, improve vibrations, and set intentions. Blue Moons are also a good time for truth seeking, meditation, love spells, divination work, protection, wishes, and banishing. The Goddesses most associated with a Blue Moon are Hathor, Artemis, Luna, Isis, Astarte, Diana, and Selene.

Shakespeare was the one who came up with "Blue Moon." Depending on the type of culture you grew up in, the Blue Moon could be tricky and mysterious. Other people think that his time is lucky. But the fun thing to look at is what some of the old wives' used to say about it. Let's take a quick look at some Blue Moon superstitions:

1. Working spells for fertility during the day before, of, and after the Blue Moon gives them more power.

2. Pick berries and flowers during a Blue Moon for abundance and love. You can also dry and label these to use in the future.

3. Native Americans view a Blue Moon as a time of change.

4. The energy of the Blue Moon can help you with your goals, which include finding a job, figuring out legal problems, exciting travel, and improving finances. You can also place objects that represent any of these goals on your altar under the Moon.

5. If a Blue Moon happens during an eclipse, when you do good deeds, you will get that back in your life. This is also the best time to resolve feuds.

6. Turning a coin that is in your pocket during a Blue Moon will give you more luck and fortune.

7. Teachers of the Islamic faith suggest praying for a person's well being during a Blue Moon.

As you can see, a lot of this works into Wicca, and you can use some of the old wisdom to improve your practice. Now, let's take a look at some Blue Moon magic that you can have ready the next time a Blue Moon rises.

Cleansing Ritual

To get ready for your ritual, you will want to cleanse yourself. You can do this however you would like. You can take a simple shower or bath, or you can do something more special.

You are going to need:

- Paper

- White candle

- Matches or lighter

- Pen

- Black thread

Decide of you are going to do this inside or outside. Doing it outside has an amazing effect on this spell. If you do it inside, try to do it close to a window that can be opened up as it will sometimes get a bit smoky.

Once you are clean and have everything ready, spend some time focusing on your breathing. Release things that could be bothering you so that you can give your ritual all of your attention. Now, light your candle. Take some time to watch as the flame moves.

If you want, this would be the time to call the elements and your chosen deities.

Now, take your paper and do some free writing. Write down anything that has been troubling you as of late. Pour all of your feelings out on the piece of paper. There is no need to worry about if it is legible, spelled correctly, or makes sense. Just write things down. The paper can hold these things. You can use as many sheets as you need.

Once you are done writing, roll the paper up into a tight scroll. If you want to use some related herbs, place them in the center of the paper before rolling it up. Tie the black thread around it to keep it tight.

Get to where you are under the light of the Moon. If you are outside, you don't need to move. Inside, you can stand next to a window and poke out your arm or face. Take some deep breaths, and while you are exhaling, feel all of these worries slipping away.

Light the paper and watch while it burns. While it is burning, picture all the darkness flowing out of you and into the Earth, anything else that helps you picture yourself releasing your worries. At this point, you can do whatever feels right to you. You can chant, dance, sing, drum, play music, or whatever feels right to you.

If at any point the paper stops burning, light it again and let it burn out completely. The ashes or small bits that are left on the plate can be buried or given to a plant.

It is now time to end the ritual. Do this by thanking and saying goodbye to any elements or deities that you called. You can add in any closing words that you want at this point. If you can, allow the candle to burn out as you meditate in the afterglow of your ritual.

Blue Moon Beauty Spell

This is a great spell if you have been focusing on your flaws. This will help you to feel confident and see yourself as a beautiful person.

You are going to need:

- Any black crystal

- Purple candle

- Bowl of water

- Lavender oil

Begin by lighting your candle and dropping some of the lavender oil into the bowl of water. Place the crystal into the water. Take some time and center yourself. Take some deep breaths, and meditate for a few minutes. When you feel ready, say:

"I am filled with beauty, from head to toe. This beauty remains forever. It will only continue to grow. I will fight forever to protect it. It is a fire within me that will forever remain free."

Say this as many times as you need to. It will continue to intensify the more you say it. Believe the words you are saying. Once you feel ready, take the crystal out of the water. Keep this crystal with you and use it for self-love. Let the candle burn out.

Blue Moon Money Spell

A Blue Moon is a great time to perform money spells. It helps you to set intentions for wealth and good fortune while also opening you up to prosperity and abundance. If you really want to harness the power of the Moon, you can time your casting to just after midnight before the Moon reaches its peak.

You are going to need:

- Dried bay leaf

- Matches

- Statue of your chosen lunar deity

- Pen

At midnight on the night of the Blue Moon, place the statue on your altar. Take some time to think about the money that you want. Hold the bay leaf in the palm of your hand and begin to visualize different ways of getting that money. Try to think up at least five ways that you could get this kind of money. Really think about the amount of money you want and think about how it makes you feel.

Now, on the bay leaf, write down the amount of money that you want. Hold the leaf again and breathe. Now light a match and burn the leaf as you focus on the money. As the smoke begins to rise, ask out loud for the money.

Blue Moon Happiness Spell

If you are looking to add happiness into your life and make others around you happy, then this is the perfect spell to do.

You are going to need:

- Clear quartz

- Bowl of water

- Orange candle

- Citrus oil

Begin by lighting your candle. Drop some of the citrus oil into the water. There is no exact amount, just as much as you think you need to. Put your quartz into the water. Now, take a moment to clear out your energy, so take a few deep breaths and allow yourself to become present in the moment. Once you feel sufficiently cleared and centered, say:

"There is a bright light surrounding me and all of my loved ones. We are protected; we are blessed. Nothing can stop us."

While you are doing this, picture the light of the Moon surrounding you and everyone you care about. Visualize it as much and as deeply as you can. Once you feel ready, take the quartz out of the water and then hold it whenever you need to feel happy. Let the candle burn out.

Moonlit Walk

This is a very simple ritual that you can do during a Blue Moon. Take a walk beneath the Blue Moon and allow all of its vibrations to wash over you. This could also be used as the start of a ritual or spell to help cleanse you.

Chapter 5: Casting Circles

Casting circles is one of the basic skills used in witchcraft. It often the first thing that beginners will learn. The idea of casting circles is a bit complex, even if the techniques tend to be simple.

Casting a circle or circle-casting is the practice of creating a temporary space to perform a ritual or magic. By definition, it is round. While circle-casting is most commonly used by Wiccans, other Witches from different religions cast circles as well. The circle is a temporary temple, an area away from the ordinary world that can hold the magic you are working.

Typically, a circle is cast at the beginning of a rite by the high priestess and/or priest. Solitary practitioners are able to cast circles as well. After the spellwork is done and the ritual is completed, the circle is released.

The circle is not a physical, but psychic boundary. It is not felt or seen by your regular senses. However, a circle can be detected energetically. It is also believed that this circle extends throughout all worlds and not just within our physical plane.

Why Should I Cast a Circle?

There are many different things that can interfere with your magic. Chaotic entities that feed your power, people with contrary wills, distractions from the world, are a few things that can interfere. Having a circle casting is one way to help shut out these influences and keep yourself focused. A magical trance can be psychically vulnerable, so a lot of witches will cast a circle to help protect their minds.

The outer barrier isn't the only important barrier of the circle. The inner barrier is just as important. Magical energy often bounces around and scatters throughout the Universe. The point of performing magic and rituals is to concentrate your energy on a purpose. Having a circle will allow you to gather more energy and hold onto it. If you call upon certain deities or spirits, a circle will offer them a cozy place to be during your rite.

So, you could say that a circle is meant to keep disturbances out and energy in. While this is very much a simplification, it is an easy way to look at it. It can also be viewed as a tool to improve the strength of your magic.

Do I Have to Cast a Circle?

You do not have to cast a circle. Not every tradition uses a circle. Egyptian, Norse, and other folk and shamanic magic practitioners work will without one. It is simply a useful technology and not a hard-and-fast rule.

How Big and What Shape Should My Circle Be?

The traditional size for a Wiccan circle is nine feet in diameter. Nine, or three times three, is a very important thing in Wicca. In many traditions, and within most covens, they will have a ritual nine-foot cord. They fold it in half and anchor it in the center and walk around in a circle to trace the circle's edge

Now, that's not to say you have to have a nine-foot circle. This is simply a suggestion. You can tailor your circle to the space you have available. You can make it too small, though.

To figure out if it is too small, gather your spell tools and yourself in the space you were thinking about using. If the circle you cast is so small that you could accidentally penetrate its edges while gesturing or reaching for something, then it is too small. Now, if the circle is being cast for a coven, the circle should be big enough so that everybody can maintain a comfortable distance from one another.

If, like most solitary practitioners, you only have a bedroom or study of some sort to work your magic in, a nine-foot circle is definitely not practical. It is better to have a smaller circle than a large circle that extends through furniture and walls.

68

You typically don't want anything more in your circle than you, your altar, and tools for your spell work.

Casting Your Circle

It is always good to check and double check to make sure that you have everything with you before you cast your circle. Have your altar set up, your book of shadows with you, all of your spell and ritual tools, and anything else you may need in your space before you start casting your circle. Most people do not want to walk through their circle to get something once it has been cast. That said, if an emergency arises and you do need to leave quickly, then do so. Nothing catastrophic is going to happen if you leave your circle before closing your circle. A child and pet can also walk through your circle, and it won't disrupt anything.

Also, some people will draw a "door" if they need to leave their circle before their spellwork is finished using a wand or athame. You can also pretend that there is a "curtain" there that you walk through. When you reenter your circle, simply walk around the edge in a clockwise circle to help strengthen it again.

One last note before we jump into the circle casting methods, there are two words that you need to learn that may show up in some spells. The first is deosil. Deosil means clockwise.

The second is widdershins. Widdershins means counterclockwise.

Simple Circle Cast

To begin, you will need to mark your circle. You first need to figure out where you want your circle to be. It doesn't matter if you are using the space where your altar is, doing it outside, or in your bedroom, you want to make sure it is somewhere you aren't going to be disturbed.

While you don't have to, some people will physically mark their circles with something meaningful. You can use a cord, crystals, or candles to mark your circle. You can also use crystals that correspond with the cardinal point.

Next, you will need to conjure up some energy that is going to protect and surround you and your work. Place yourself in the middle of what will be your circle. Allow yourself to relax and take a few deep breaths. Imagine that the top of your head is starting to open up like a funnel to take in a divine, white light. This is the crown of your head is will always have a strong connection with the Divine. You can open this up and amplify it whenever you want.

Bring your arms out so that your palms are facing out. Every time you take a breath in, picture yourself pulling all of that light into your crown, and every time you breathe out, push the light out through your palms to surround you with a protective shield. As your space fills with all of this energy, you may notice that you start to buzz or tingle, develop goosebumps, or feel uplifted.

Using the arm you write with, stretch it out to the side and point to the edge of your circle. Spin, three times, in a clockwise direction as you mentally mark your circle using this divine light. Bring both hands above your head and say: "I ask that the God and Goddess bless this circle so that I might be free and protected within this space. So mote it be."

Your circle is now cast; you can start to perform your ritual or cast spells. To close this circle, simply spin counterclockwise and feel the protective light dissipate.

Advanced Circle Casting

You'll need a compass and four candles. The four candles can be all white, or you can have one blue, one red, one yellow, and one green.

To start, take your compass and find the four cardinal points. Put the candles at each of these points. If you have the colored candles, the green one goes at North, yellow at East, red at South, and blue and West.

Begin at the North candle, light it, and repeat: "Guardians of the North, element of Earth, I call upon thee to be present during this ritual. Please join me now and bless this circle."

Move to the East candle, light it, and repeat: "Guardians of the East, element of Air, I call upon thee to be present during this ritual. Please join me now and bless this circle."

Move to the South candle, light it, and repeat: "Guardians of the South, element of Fire, I call upon thee to be present during this ritual. Please join me now and bless this circle."

Move to the West candle, light it, and repeat: "Guardians of the West, element of Water, I call upon thee to be present during this ritual. Please join me now and bless this circle."

Take your wand or athame and point it towards the edge of your circle. Walk in a clockwise direction three times and picture a white light rushing into the crown of your and being pushed out through your arm and through your tool, to the edge of your circle.

Take your place in the middle of the circle and feel your circle being filled with divine light. Say: "God and Goddess, guardian angels, and spiritual guides, please be present with me during this ritual. Bless this circle and keep me protected. No unwanted entities are welcome here; only pure, divine beings are invited into this space. This circle is cast. So mote it be."

You can now start your ritual and spellwork. When closing the circle, make sure you blow out your candles in the opposite order you lit them and thank the elements for being present.

Circle Casting

This is a rather simple circle casting, but you are going to need three, four, six, or nine things of a certain object. You can pick whichever number and whichever item resonates with you, but each other should be objects that are similar. For example, you could use four houseplants, nine candles, three rocks, or six seashells. If you have any sacred items, feel free to use those.

To cast your circle, start by holding your objects in your hands and create the intention for them as you move around your circle and place them to mark off the edge of your circle. If you are using candles, you will want to make sure that you have them placed on something safe so that you can light them safely without them catching something on Fire.

If you feel there are some words you would like to say as you do this, you can do it now, but this circle casting does not require that. Once you have placed all of your items, you are free to do your spell or ritual work.

To close this circle, all you need to do is pick your items in the opposite direction that you placed them.

Closing Your Circle

Once all of the work has been done, you will need to close your circle. When you release your circle, it gives the energies within a chance to dissipate and the room to return to its pre-ritual state. There are many different ways to close your circle, like ringing a bell, performing the casting in reverse, or picturing the walls dissolving. Gathering up your tools and putting them away will also help to scatter out the energy.

If you forget to close your circle, or you simply don't close it well, the circle will eventually fade on its own in a few minutes or hours. If you regularly use that area for your ritual work, then it may slow down the dissipation. That doesn't mean you should make it a habit to just walk away. You should always close your circle.

Chapter 6: The Magic Within the Flame

A lot of people believe that candle magic is the oldest form of magic. Whether or not that is true does not matter. What is true is that Fire has always been scared to humans, especially our pagan ancestors. They would honor their Gods with candles, torches, flaming wheels, and balefires. Since Fire was the main source of light, next to the Moon and Sun, until around the early 1900s, it is very easy to see why Fire has always been a symbol of power.

This reverence for Fire has continued even after modern lighting became a thing. Most religions will still use candles as a part of their service in some way. Candle magic is also the easiest way to cast spells and doesn't take as many ritual or ceremonial tools. Basically, any person with a candle has the ability to cast a spell. Think about your birthdays. You make a wish when you blow out your candles. This is basically the same idea as candle magic. Instead of "hoping" that you wish comes true, candle magic means you declare your intent. Nobody is certain where this tradition came from, but it has been a tradition that has stayed the course.

There is also something very calming about the flicker of the candle flame. It helps us to feel peaceful and at ease when we gaze into that dancing, flickering light. Lighting a candle is an easy way to begin shifting from your regular reality and connecting to the unseen energies that surround us. It doesn't matter if you plan on casting a spell or not.

Candle spells tend to be very straightforward, simple, and elegant. They are a great way to strengthen and build your "magic muscles" or to improve your ability to direct and focus energy into an intention. The powerful thoughts are what underlie the simplest and complex forms of magic.

Why Candle Magic?

People new to magic may have this notion that they can get more from a complicated spell, but that's not true. Candle magic may be simple, but it is a very powerful form of magic. The reason for this is that it harnesses transformative power through the flame, wax, and wick.

Whenever you perform candle magic, you are harnessing the power of Fire in order to bring about change. Think about all of the things that Fire can change. In candle, it melts the wax. It is able to turn organic materials like bone, flesh, wood, and leaves into ash. It is able to soften hard metals. It can heat things up and change a liquid into a gas. Fire helps to transform dough into a loaf of bread or batter into a cake. It can also provide your warmth during the cold months of winter, and light during the dark night.

Ever since humans discovered Fire, we have been in awe of its power. We have long tried to harness its power to use it for transformative magic. We continue to do this through candle magic. The second you start to plan out a spell, you have begun the process of casting. You should make sure that your intentions remain good since you are pouring your energy into your goal. The candle itself isn't the power source. Instead, it is the Fire that burns the wick and melts the wax that is driving force.

Also, a candle is one of the best examples of all of the elements working together in one place. The base and wick of the candle represents the Earth. These are needed to keep the flame lit and the candle grounded. The wax transforms from a solid to liquid and then to a gas, which is representative of Water. Air is found in the oxygen which the flame needs in order to stay lit. Of course, the flame is Fire. You can also see the element of Spirit when it comes to you charging your candle with a certain intention. You now have a tool that embodies the whole Universe in a simple little package.

Candle Safety

There will be a lot of spells that will ask you to let your candles burn out completely. It is never a good idea to leave a burning candle unattended. But, if you need to, make sure that it is placed in a flame proof container away from anything that is flammable. You also want to make sure that it is sitting on something solid and can't easily be knocked over. You should also be mindful of what anointing oils you use because they can be flammable, and you don't want to end up burning your fingers.

Make sure that your candle is in a proper holder when you are letting it burn out. It could end up going out before the entire candle has burned away, or it could melt into nothingness. Either way is fine, and you should not relight the candle.

Once the candle has done what it is going to do, you can bury the remnants outsides to finish your spell.

Chapter 7: Selecting Your Candles

You might have noticed that flames and fire usually accompany many prayers and rituals. Fire has always been a huge part of most ceremonies and traditions. Since ancient times, candles have been used to light their altars. You should never underestimate the spiritual and magical powers of candles. When you light a candle, it exerts magic and creates an environment that is spiritual. Candle spells and candle magic are a powerful type of magic that seems subtle but can have powerful implications.

Candle Magic and Spells

Candles are important for most rituals and spells. Their colors and shapes are also important when doing Wiccan rituals, Voodoo, Witchcraft, and magic. The way you cleanse, dress, and charge them along with their colors and being able to create enough energy is critical to your magic and spells actually working.

Different Candles and Their Use

There are many different types of candles that are specific for effects and functions, and each one has been assigned to a specific spell. Some types might include Zodiac candles, seven-day candles, shaped, and pillars. Pillar candles are the most common and can be used daily. They come in a variety of colors and are used because they last a long time. Each candle has a specific use. Chakra candles get used to cleanse our bodies and to provide holistic effects. The shaped ones are used to cast certain types of spells.

- Devil-Be-Gone and Satan

These are in the shape of the Christian's devil and can be used to remove spirits, negative energies, entities, and exorcisms. Burn it with an astral candle to represent someone who needs to be cleansed.

- Crucifix or Cross

These candles can be used for banishing spells or for protection. They are also very beneficial when used as an offering to Lwa, a saint, God, deities, or Orisha.

- Scented Candles

You can use scented candles in your spells. Below you will find a list that shows you the magical properties of each scent:

  o Patchouli: attracts money

  o Pine: gets rid of negative energy, strength

  o Rose: love

- o Sandalwood: protections, healing, purification

- o Strawberry: love, friendship, luck

- o Tangerine: prosperity

- o Vanilla: sexual passion, enhance memory

- o Blueberry: keeps negative energy away

- o Myrrh: purification, protection

- o Carnation: healing

- o Musk: strength, love, sexual passion, courage

- o Cherry: attracts love

- o Lotus: harmony, inner peace

- o Cinnamon: good fortune, attracts wealth

- o Jasmine: love

- o Coconut: purification, protection

- o Honeysuckle: healing, psychic abilities, good luck

- o Frangipani: attracts positive energy

- Jumbo, Pillar, and Altar

These candles are tall and thick. They burn very slowly. This is why they are great to be used as deity or altar candles because they get lit first but extinguished last. These can be found in glass containers as seven-day candles.

- Eve and Adam

These are in the shape of a nude female and male. You can find them in many colors. They are used in attraction and love spells. You can use them to bring love to your life, to bring back a lost love, push away unwanted love, or to break up relationships.

- Seven-Knob

These candles consist of seven evenly sized knobs. You can burn one knob every day while you focus on your goals, desires, and wishes. Because it takes seven days to completely burn an entire candle, it makes your magic very potent. The following list will let you know what color to burn according to your desires:

- o Red: putting energy in motion, getting rid of obstacles, love spells

- o Orange: getting rid of obstacles and business success

- o Yellow: removing bad luck

- Green: court case spells, manifesting, money spells

- Blue: confusion, fights, stop depression

- Purple: spiritual protection and defeating spiritual attacks

- White: granting secret wishes, purification

- Black: releasing spells, banishing spells

- Brown: justice spells

- Cat

These will be in the shape of a cat, obviously. Use a black one to break jinxes, hexes, and to break curses. They can be used to attract good luck and to get rid of bad luck. A green one can help with healing and prosperity, especially if you are trying to heal your pet. If you want to increase the potency of love spells, use a red one.

- Zodiac or Astral

These candles can represent another person or yourself in a ritual or spell. They have many uses and could be used in various rituals. Be sure that you never throw them away. You need to always allow them to burn out completely or store them safely. Use the color chart below to help with your spells:

- o Aries: white, red, pink

- o Taurus: green yellow, red, pink

- o Gemini: yellow, blue, red, silver

- o Leo: green red, orange, gold

- o Scorpio: brown, black, red

- o Cancer: green, brown, white

- o Virgo: grey, black, yellow, gold

- o Libra: black, light brown, blue

- o Sagittarius: blue, gold, red, purple

- o Pisces: green, blue, white

- o Capricorn: brown, red, black

- o Aquarius: green, blue

- Table

These candles can be found in most stores and can be used in most rituals. Try to find the best quality and be sure they haven't been dipped.

- Skull and Mummy

Skull candles look like skulls, and mummy candles look like mummies lying in a coffin. These candles offer protection and are great when warding off death, illness, and dangerous situations.

- Taper

These candles are thin and tall, and you have to be careful when dressing and anointing them. These are best when quick results are needed. Make sure you always use a holder and be sure the one you get is colored all the way through and not just the outside.

Using Colors for Spells

The color of the candle can play an important role since color brings its own energy and power. This is why it is important to choose the right color for the purpose of the spell and your intention. The following show what every color symbolizes and stand for along with their magical properties.

- Red

This is the color of health, vigor, passion, and energy. Red candles can be used to perform spells to bring back a lost love, family relationships, friendships, self love, and romantic love.

This is the color of vitality and health. It strengthens and inflames the soul and protects against corrupt or negative influences. Red is the color o sexual prowess and passion. This color has been associated with Fire. If you light a candle before a task that takes courage along with a heart that is steadfast like a first date or interview.

- Orange

This is the color of attention and energy. Burn it to attract objects or influences. Any spell that was designed to locate anything that was lost might call for using an orange candle. You can combine it with other colors to strengthen its powers. Orange stands for encouragement, thinking clearly, happiness, physical energy, and stimulating a positive mind. It can be used in spells for setting goals, creativity, and courage.

- Yellow

This is the color of knowledge and discovery. It can improve your range of motion and imagination. This color has been associated with Air. If you light a yellow candle before you start studying, it can help improve your recollection. It is very useful to a person who is serious about their magic. Shades of yellow could range from lime yellow, golden sunflower, and non-metallic yellow. It stands for charming, attraction, and cheerfulness. It can be used in rituals to make your dreams come true, such as getting your hands on money.

- Green

This is the color of luck, money, fortune, growth, and prosperity. It has been associated with healing. It is commonly associated with Earth. Light one before beginning a task involving money, like looking for a new job. Green is the color of harvest, financial and business success, money, and wealth. Use green candles when you are casting spells to achieve financial or business success.

- Blue

This is the color of relaxation and happiness. It can promote healing and can strengthen your psychic link to the spiritual realm. It can be used for learning spells, solving problems, and communicating. If you don't sleep well, project a desire to sleep better into a blue candle that has been lit for a few moments before you get into bed. Make sure you extinguish it before you go to sleep. Blue candles can enhance your spiritual awareness. Use light blue instead of dark blue as they are more uplifting.

1. Dark blue: these symbolize extensive and deep mental thought and true devotion toward spirituality. These

candles can be used for spells that are cast to make people moody or depressed.

2. Medium blue: these will symbolize peace and spiritual fortitude.

3. Light blue: these stand for calmness, perception, clarity in thinking, tranquility, and coolness.

- Violet or Purple

This is the color of power. Blue can increase your psychic awareness, and violet can increase your magical powers. Burn one with other colors to make your spells more potent. When you are casting a healing spell, burn a violet one with a blue one; violet will strengthen your desire to cast a healing spell. It can be used in spells relating to increasing your spiritual connections, clairvoyance, confidence, and intuition.

- White

This is the color of unity and purity. The color white contains every color. It has been associated with truth, spirituality, and illumination. White candles are frequently used in purification and defense rituals, along with peace, success, and abundance spells. You can light them if you think you might come in contact with things that are unclean or dark temptations. White stands for power, innocence, and spiritual strength. It can also be used to forge connections with departed loved ones, getting rid of destructive energies, and contacting your spirit guides. If you aren't sure about what color you should use, always go for white.

- Pink

This is the color of connections. It is representative of communication and nurturing that is important to love like a person's looks or magnetism. It can help bolster confidence. If you light a pink candle before your ceremony, it will emphasize the connection between people, like someone getting married. Pink candles represent romance, affection, and love and are used to cast spells for meaningful and long lasting relationships.

- Silver

Silver is great to get rid of and dissolve all negativity and to emerge victoriously. It represents good that overtakes everything evil. It could be viewed as a different shade of white. Silver can be used for lunar connections, intuition, and reflection. Silver helps remove destructive forces and negative powers. It can neutralize negative situations. It helps develop psychic powers. Silver has been associated with the powers of the female deity.

- Brown

This represents the natural world, particularly animals. You can combine this color with other colors to push your spells toward the natural world rather than yourself or others. Medium brown can pause actions and stands for being hesitant. Russet brown has some influences of red and stands for uncertainty in love and romance.

- Gold

This isn't the same as yellow. Gold candles are used for solar connections, business endeavors, and financial gain. They can help with intuition, divination, great fortune, financial gains, and prosperity. Gold is great to attract healing, happiness, influence, money, and knowledge. Gold has been associated with the powers of the male deity.

Chapter 8: Preparing Your Candles

You are going to need to cleanse your candles to get rid of all energies that might have been infused into them while they were being manufactured, while on the shelf or a story, after it has been burned in a different room, or burned for a different purpose. You will need to cleanse your candles if you don't make them yourself while infusing them with a specific spell. Here are some ways you can cleanse your candles:

- Place your candle outside or on a windowsill where it will be in direct moonlight overnight.

- Make a bowl of sea salt and bury the candle in it for 24 hours.

- Burn sage, incense, or Palo Santo and pass the candle through the smoke.

- Saturate a cotton ball in rubbing alcohol and rub it over the surface of the candle. Move it from bottom to top to expel its energy.

Now that you know how to cleanse your candles, the next steps are anointing and then inscribing them. These aren't as complicated as they sound, and they add a lot of power to your spells and rituals. Now all spells will require you to anoint or inscribe your candle, but some will.

If you are working a love or attraction spell to try and find love or strengthen a relationship you already have, then you would want a pink candle, or red, and inscribe it with love base symbols. Once you inscribe it, you would then bless, or anoint the candle with a love or attraction oil.

The same is true for a wealth or prosperity spell and ritual. You would use a green candle and then inscribe symbols and words that represent wealth and prosperity on it and then anoint it with prosperity oils.

Inscribing

The first thing you need to do after you have cleansed it is to inscribe the candle. It is easier to inscribe before you anoint the candle because the candle is going to be slippery once it is anointed with oils. You would use symbols, sigils, or words that represent whatever it is your spell or ritual is about.

For example, if a person is performing a love spell and you want to be loved by a person that you know, you can carve their initials and your initials into the candle. You can also use their full name as well. You can also use other symbols that represent love if you want, like hearts or ancient love symbols.

Having something with a fine point to scratch across the surface is the best for inscribing. You can use a safety pin, a special scribing tool, and you can even use an athame. Once you have picked the item you want to inscribe with, dedicate it solely for that purpose and use it only for that.

The things you can inscribe into your candle are endless. You can even come up with a sigil that represents your intention for your spell. To create a sigil, all you need to do is to write a sentence that is your intention, such as "I want to bring a passionate lover into my life." Then you would go through and get rid of all the vowels. This is going to give you "wnttbrngpssntlvrntmylf." Now you need to go through and get rid of any repeating letters. This brings you to: "wntbrgpslvmt." You now take those letters and smoosh them together however you see fit into a witchy looking symbol. There is no right or wrong way to draw a sigil.

Whenever you inscribe your candles, you want to visualize the outcome you want from your spell. If should be its own ritual. After you have inscribed your candle, you can then "dress" it if you want to.

Anointing

Anointing your candles can help you properly charge them. You need to anoint the candle with oils that correspond with your desired outcomes. There are even some spells that call for bodily fluids to anoint the candles.

How to anoint your candle will sometimes vary between sources. In general, most people will hold their candle in one hand and then coat their first two fingers in the oil and then draw a line from the top of the candle down to the middle. Some will do this all the way around the candle, and then they will turn the candle and so the same from the bottom to the center. This will cover the candle completely in the oil.

As you are anointing your candle, think about the outcome you want to get from your spell. People will normally anoint their candles in a certain direction, depending on the spell they are doing. For spells that are helping you to attract something, you would anoint from top to middle and bottom to middle. If you are trying to send something away, then you would anoint it from the center to the top and then center to bottom.

Some people will do a single stroke from top to bottom to attract things, and then from the bottom to the top to get rid of things. Some people refer to covering the entire candle in oil as consecrating, and when they do this, they simply rub the oil all over the candle instead of worrying about doing it in a certain direction.

Despite the fact that there are conflicting methods of anointing a candle, you really can't go wrong with it as long as you have a strong intention.

After you have anointed your candle in oil, you can then anoint it with herbs, too. You don't have to do both. It is pretty much just a matter of preference. Again, make sure that they correspond with the purpose of your spell.

We're going to go over the oils and their purpose, but if you can't find some of the oils mentioned below for love spells, you can always use lavender or rose oil because they can be used for all love spells, even if they are meant to break people up. The only difference would be the direction you anoint them.

- Harmony: ylang-ylang, gardenia

- Money: heliotrope, vetiver, bergamot, honeysuckle, peppermint, cinnamon, jasmine

- Strength: carnation

- Healing: gardenia, myrrh, carnation, frankincense, clove, lavender, cedar

- Protection: heliotrope, violet, juniper, rosemary, lilac, pine, bayberry, patchouli, myrrh, carnations, frankincense, dragon's blood

- Curse and hex removal: myrrh, cedar, yarrow, dragon's blood, vetiver

- Prosperity: musk, bayberry

- Balance: magnolia

- Happiness: bergamot, amber, gardenia

- Purification and cleansing: frankincense, sage, cedar, sandalwood, dragon's blood, patchouli

- Fertility: rose

- Control: bayberry

- Energy: peppermint, cinnamon, rosemary

- Creativity: peppermint, clove

- Dreams: jasmine

- Love: lavender and rose can be used for all

  o Have someone fall in love: musk, violet, jasmine, lavender

- o True love: ylang-ylang, rose

- o Attract love: patchouli, gardenia, amber

- o Lust and sex: orange, nutmeg, musk

- o Break up: columbine

- o Remove problems: Melissa

- o Commitment: patchouli, rose

- o Faithful: magnolia

- Psychic abilities and divination: jasmine, yarrow, honeysuckle, myrrh

If you do want to use herbs as well as oil, you can use the same list for the herbs. All you would need to do is once it has been anointed, is roll the candle in the herbs. They will stick to the oil easily. When a candle is dressed, you will want to really watch it when it burns because it can pop and spark more than normal.

Chapter 9: Candle Spells

Here you will find your first candle spells. These are all fairly simple spells that even beginners can do.

Potion for Dreams

This spell is meant to help provide you with dreams from your spirit guides, or any other power you would like to get guidance from. This should be done 30 to 60 minutes before you plan on going to sleep, and make sure you have a journal next to your bed.

You are going to need:

- Light or matches

- Water

- Athame or wand

- Graveyard dirt – you can also use dirt from a place that you feel a connection with, or you can omit this ingredient

- Lavender oil

- A cauldron

- Black tealight candle

Add water to the cauldron that equals about a half of a cup. You don't have to measure it. You can eyeball it. Sprinkle the dirt inside and then say what your intention is. It works best if you come up with your own intention, but to give you an idea, you could say: "A bit of dirt to bring me closer to a world full of luster."

Stir some of the lavender oil into the water. Light the candle and put it underneath your cauldron. You will need to have your cauldron on a stand so that the candle simply sits under it so that the flame warms the bottom of the cauldron. You will start to smell the potion as it heats up. Let your muscles relax and allow your thoughts to start drifting around.

Sit with your cauldron until the candle has burned all the way out, the water evaporates, or you feel as if the spell is finished. Make sure you record any dreams that you have as you sleep that night.

Fix a Friendship Spell

You are going to need:

- Ground dry basil

- White candle

- Thin lavender candle

You will want to be patient with this spell because it can be tricky to put together. Crack the lavender candle in the middle but keep the wick intact. This crack represents the rift between you and another person that you are trying to fix. As you perform this spell, focus on this problem that you would like to overcome and how you could help to improve things between the two of you if you were given a chance.

Rub a bit of basil on the rough ends of the broken spot of the lavender candle then push them back together. Light the white candle and allow the wax to drip over the broken piece until the lavender candle has been mended back together.

Sit the lavender in a holder and light it. Let it burn until the flame gets close to where the break is. Now, sit with the candle and watch the flame as it burns through the joined break, thinking about different ways to improve your relationship. Once it has moved through the split, let the candle continue to burn out all on its own.

Spell for Abundance

You are going to need:

- Large denomination coin

- Vanilla essential oil

- Cinnamon essential oil

- Green candle

With something sharp, write "Prosperity" up the side of your candle and then anoint it with the vanilla and cinnamon oils. Place the coin inside of the holder and place the candle on top of it. Light your candle and allow it to sit and burn out completely.

Once the candle is completely burned out, leave the coin that is covered in wax in a safe place to bring more money into your life.

Blessing for Good Health

You are going to need:

- White candle

- Cinnamon stick

- Glass of apple juice

It is best if you are able to use natural, organic ingredients for this. If you can't, that's okay, just make sure that apple juice is good quality.

With the juice in a glass, take the cinnamon stick and stir it four times. Light your candle and take a couple of sips of the juice. Then say: "Lord and Lady bless the body with health and wellness."

Drink the rest of the juice and then blow the candle out. This spell can be done whenever you start to feel a little ill, or you can do it every morning.

Red Hot Love Spell

You are going to need:

- Something with a point for carving

- Lavender essential oil

- Yarrow essential oil

- Rose essential oil

- Red string or yarn

- Three taper red candles

Start out by carving a heart on each of the candles and then carve a pentacle inside each of the hearts. You don't have to do this perfectly, as long as you can tell what it is, it will be fine. Anoint each of the candles with one of the oils and then tie them together with the string or yarn so that the symbols are touching in the middle. Tie a bow into the string and then place them in a candle dish or holder.

As you light the three candles, say: "Live, life, love, I ask from above, three times three, bring them to me."

Allow all of the candles to burn a third of the way down then blow them all out. Do this same thing for the following two nights until the candles have burned all the way out. In the next few days, you will start to see signs about somebody new entering your life for romance.

Psychic Dream Spell

You need:

- Large amethyst piece

- Black marker

- Small square of silver or purple fabric

- White candle

With the marker, draw an eye onto the candle, the stone, and the fabric. Place everything onto your altar and then light your candle.

Place the stone on top of the fabric so that their eyes are touching. Picture the eye in your forehead that can be opened up to see into all of your dreams. Hold this to your forehead, with eye touching your skin.

Watch the flame of the candle, saying, "open sight" over and over again. Place the fabric and stone back on the table and then allow the candle to burn out completely. After you are finished, place the fabric under your pillow and sleep on it.

Happy Family Spell

This spell helps to ease tension in a family or any other large gathering.

You are going to need:

- Sandalwood incense

- Piece of clear quartz

- Handful of basil – fresh

- Pink candle

- Four candles of different colors

This can be done on your altar, but it is best when you can do it in a central part of your home. Place the five candles in a circle. Place the quartz in the middle and cover it with the basil leaves. Light your candles.

Light your incense and walk it through all of the main rooms in your home. Do this slowly and allow the smoke to really spread throughout. After you have done this, go back to the candles and sit the incense down. Allow everything to burn out on their own. You should notice that the tension starts to lift soon.

Improved Finance Spell

You are going to need:

- A piece of paper

- Several acorns

- Pine incense

- Patchouli incense

- A gold candle

- A green candle

Carve the rune fehu into the bottom of each of the candles. Place them in candle holders that you sit across from one another. Place the patchouli incense next to the gold candle, and the pin next to the green candle. Light the candles and start burning the incense.

Draw out another fehu on your piece of paper and place the acorns on it. If you aren't able to find acorns, you can simply use smooth stones. Allow the candles to burn out and then leave the stones or acorns on your altar until you have extra money come into your life.

Chapter 10: The Power of Crystals

You have probably held a crystal in your hand at some point in your life and looked at it from every angle. You might have even felt a mysterious power that these stones hold. They speak a silent living, creative, infinite power that lies in the Earth. Crystals have been respected for hundreds of years and have been used in jewelry and talismans since ancient times. Mineral stones and crystals have been used for many magical purposes, bringing energy into your physical space, and for healing. Let's learn the basics of crystals.

What Are Crystals?

In many "new age" and Wiccan circles, the word "crystal" talks about a large variety of minerals, and many of them aren't even true crystals. All of them fall under the crystal umbrella.

A simple definition of a mineral is "any inorganic substance that gets formed in the Earth's underground geological processes naturally." Each mineral will have its own energy signature and chemical composition.

Most minerals are made of molecules that fit together in repeating patterns that give them their geometric forms that we think of when we hear "crystal." When crystals form, it is called crystallization. Crystals form with liquids cool and begin to harden. Specific molecules in this liquid will band together while they try to stabilize themselves. This happens in a repeating and uniform pattern that creates the crystal.

Crystals can be formed from magma, or liquid rock as it cools. If it cools very slowly, crystals will form. Very valuable crystals like rubies, emeralds, and diamonds form this way.

The most common crystal is the clear quartz. This is what a true crystal ball will be made of. Amethyst and rose quartz follow the clear quartz as the most abundant. Bloodstone, jade, and lapis lazuli are popular stones that are used in magic. These crystals are actually a combination of minerals and aren't considered to be true crystals. Some crystals like jet and amber are actually organic substances that have been fossilized. In order to keep things simple, many people who work with these gifts use the words "stones" and "crystals" interchangeably.

How Crystals Form

As stated above, crystals are a solid whose components like ions, molecules, or atoms get arranged in a very organized structure that forms a lattice that goes in every direction.

Macroscopic crystals are normally identified by their shapes and consist of flat faces with specific orientations.

The process of growing crystals through mechanisms is called solidification or crystallization. The word crystal comes from the Ancient Greek word kruos, which means "icy cold, frost," and from crustallos that means both "rock crystal" and "ice."

Most of the minerals do occur in nature as crystals. Each crystal will have an internal pattern of atoms that have a certain way they lock new atoms into patterns that repeat over and over again. The resulting crystal's shape like a hexagon or cube will mirror the internal make up of the atoms. While a crystal grows, changes in chemical composition and temperature could create some interesting variations. Students aren't going to find that perfect mineral crystal in their backyard. This is due to the fact that for a crystal to form perfect geometric surfaces and forms, crystals have to have the perfect growing conditions and enough room to grow. If many crystals grow close to each other, they might mesh together to create a conglomerated mass. This is what happens to many rocks like granite that is created from many tiny crystals. Specimens that you see in museums are grown in environments that give them the room to grow, so they form the perfect geometric shapes.

The way atoms arrange themselves inside will determine the mineral's physical and chemical properties, and this includes its color. Light will interact with various atoms to make different colors. Most minerals are colorless if found in their pure state, but impurities in the atomic structure could cause a change in color. Quartz is normally void of color but it can be found in colors from brown to pink to the deepest purple found in amethyst. It just depends on the type and number of impurities within the structure. When quartz is in its normal colorless shape, it will look like ice. The Ancient Greeks thought that clear quartz was actual ice that was frozen to the extent that it couldn't melt.

Scientists normally describe a crystal as "growing," even if they really aren't alive. Under the Earth's surface, they bristle and branch into trillions of atoms that connect into three-dimensional patterns. Every crystal will begin small but will grow larger as more atoms are added. Some will grow from water that is rich in minerals that have dissolved. They could grow from vapor and melted rock. Because of the influences of various pressures and temperatures, atoms can combine to form wonderful arrays of crystal shapes. It is because of all the perfection of symmetry and form that has drawn scientists to look at and study minerals. Symmetry can be found everywhere in nature – the beautiful wings on a butterfly, the petals of a sunflower, a snowflake, and minerals aren't an exception. These repeated patterns happen within the basic structure and will reflect this pattern of the crystal's faces. You can see the symmetry of a crystal with your eye, but if the crystal is too small, you will have to look through a microscope or magnifying glass. Seeing the patterns of crystals might be hard at first, but as you get more experienced, the more symmetry in the crystals, you will be able to recognize. Some minerals don't have crystals that are well formed and are a bit hard for experts to classify.

Crystals' Powers

Even though they are classified as inorganic, crystals are understood by most healers and Witches to be living because they give healing energy to plants, animals, and people. Specific crystals like tourmaline and quarts exhibit a power that scientists call "the piezoelectric effect." When pressure is applied to these stones, like being tapped with a hammer or squeezing them, they will give off an electric charge. Crystals like quartz exhibit a pyroelectricity. This means they release an electric charge when they get exposed to a temperature change.

Crystals are made up of minerals that are in a structured, geometric pattern. They have been classified according to their internal structures. It is their geometrical structure that gives them the healing and magical properties.

The crystal's power comes from its internal geometry. To be able to completely understand this, you have to understand sacred geometry. This is a philosophical and mathematical field that looks at the proportions and geometrical shapes within the Universe. These can be found anywhere in the world. It can be found in man-made buildings and nature. According to this, every geometric shape will vibrate with its own frequency, and this gives them their specific energetic properties. The symbols vary and are numerous: the pentacle, the triskele, the flower of life, and the Fibonacci spiral, just to name a few.

Because gemstones are arranged naturally in a geometric pattern, sacred geometry will also apply to them. This theory is the core of crystal magic. This is why we build grids using geometric shapes.

Now that you know about sacred geometry, it will help you understand how and why crystals work. Every crystal will vibrate at a frequency that is unique to its internal structure. These vibrations will affect the crystal's energy in ways that science can't explain. Because we are energy, we can be affected by crystals. Because crystals vibrate at high frequencies, they naturally store information. This is why quartz and selenite are used in electronic devices. With intentions, we can program and charge crystals so that they can help us manifest our goals. They are batteries that help power our intentions. This makes them perfect for use in magic.

There are actually only a few crystals that are popular enough to be used in magic and healing that has shown these effects during scientific studies. Normal science hasn't discovered what alternative healing practitioners have always known, and that is each crystal gives off its own energy that will interact with the energy and everything that is around it.

Witches, along with Wiccans, know that a stone or crystal's power is the same power that is in natural phenomena like a flowing river or the wind. Everything, whether invisible or visible is nothing but energy. All of that energy is connected. Because intention or thought is also energy, this too can be harnessed and sent into the Universe through the crystals that we work with. By doing this, the stones, and crystals become energy conduits. They can bring healing to us or send positive energy into the spiritual realm to manifest change in the lives of others as well as ourselves.

Magic and Rituals

Wiccans use stones and crystals to line their sacred circle before they start their ritual. They can be used to honor deities with certain stones that are sacred to certain Goddesses and Gods. Certain magical tools like pentacles and wands are sometimes decorated with crystals, and they are used in all sorts of magical jewelry.

Stone and crystals are used for all sorts of things, from manifesting love and wealth to divination to healing. Just like in ancient times, they are still being used for talismans, amulets, other charms for luck, along with protections and scrying. Crystals can add power to your spells, whether they are the main focus or as a helper ingredient of the spell.

Amethyst gets used a lot as a boost for all kinds of spells. Clear quartz is usually kept on an altar to help sharpen focus, especially if it is a very complex spell. You could also charge a certain crystal for certain purposes and carry it with you wherever you go, such as a citrine to attract money or red jasper for courage.

Crystal magic is a great way to work with colors naturally. Crystals aren't dyed like cloth or candles. Vibrant colors will resonate with various aspects of our existence, like money, health, and love, but according to their own vibrations. Pink that is found in rose quartz is great for loving vibrations, and this makes it great for bringing love to you. Green resonates with abundance and this makes bloodstone and jade great for spells that involve prosperity.

Fun Facts

- There are some living organisms that can produce crystals.

- Crystals are popular in jewelry since they come in a variety of colors and the sparkle and shine.

- Many computer screens use liquid crystals in their display.

- Diamonds are one huge molecule that is created from any atoms in one single element.

- The science of studying crystals and how they are formed is called crystallography.

Chapter 11: The Best Crystals for Magic

When it comes to using crystals in magic, it is important that you understand their correspondences. This will help you to pick out the best crystals for your spells, and to find alternatives if you can't find the crystal the spell calls for. These crystals are the most commonly used ones, and tend to be some of the easier ones to find.

Amethyst

The amethyst has been one of the most admired stones due to its legendary powers and beauty to help soothe and stimulate the emotions and mind. The ancients referred to this stone as a "gem of fire." It is connected to February, which was the month that the Romans dedicated to their God Neptune. It is also the traditional birthstone for February. It is also a faithful love stone. It has been referred to as the Bishop's Stone as well. It holds spirituality, creativity, passion, and fire, but it also bears the logic of sobriety and temperance.

Amethysts are a type of quartz crystal, and they can be found in many different locations around the globe. Manganese in clear quartz is what provides it its color, and how much iron is present will cause the various shades. You can find amethysts in shades of pale red-violet to a deep violet. It may be opaque or transparent.

Amethyst comes from ametusthos, a Greek word meaning "not intoxicated." Amethysts have long been used to prevent overindulgences and drunkenness. Ancient Romans and Greeks would put amethysts in their goblets because they thought the wine wouldn't make them drunk. Catholic bishops often wore rings with amethysts to protect them from mystical intoxication. They believed when they kissed the ring; it would help to keep them grounded.

Amethysts are a great stone to use when you are looking to be creative. It can help in things where original results are important. They have often been called the painter, poet, inventor, composer, and artist's stone.

Quartz

The clear quartz crystal is the most abundant and most common crystal in the world. It makes up the most diverse and the largest family in the mineral kingdom. Since ancient times, the clear quartz has been a light to mankind.

Most of the time, when a person uses the word crystal, they are talking about the clear quartz. Quartz are the supreme gift from Mother Earth. Even the smallest piece is filled with the properties of a master healer. The ancient people believed that these stones were alive and that they took a breath every 100 years. There are many countries who believed that they are the physical incarnation of the Divine.

Healers today still believe that the clear quartz is alive. They believe that they are wise and old and will communicate to anybody who is ready and open to receive their message. Meditating with, carrying, or wearing clear quartz can open up the heart and mind to higher guidance. It gives the spirit realm the ability to be translated and transmitted into the world physically.

Clear quartz are often used with other stones in order to amplify their energies. Clear quartz are able to produce a healing force field of negative ions as it clears out the surrounding area with positive ions. This helps to protect your aura. It helps to dispel static electricity, and helps to cancel out all of the harmful effects of radioactivity and radiation.

Jet

Jet isn't made like the other crystals we have talked about. It is formed when pieces of wood are buried, compacted, and go through an organic degradation process. Once it becomes heated, it will form a coal seam. This stone tends to be black in color, but some will appear brown. They can easily be carved or cut, and its uniform texture makes it easy to carve accurately.

They can be polished, and will have a bright shine. Jet can be found all over the US, Poland, France, Germany, Spain, India, and Russia. This stone can help to provide you with spiritual, emotional, and physical guidance that will help you to reach your goals and find harmony and balance. When paired with aragonite, it can help to show you how you can reach the top of any situation during tough times.

Jet allows you to focus on your life, relationships, and career. It can help to guide you through accomplishing your goals by using your natural abilities, skills, and talents. Jet also helps you to own up to any mistakes you make, make amends with others you have wronged, and right wrongs.

Obsidian

Obsidian is often called the mirror. If you find that you are particularly drawn to obsidian and all of its intense and mysterious vibes, it could mean that you need a psychic cleanse. It is often known as the "psychic vacuum cleaner." Obsidian helps to work as your personal spiritual maid service, and helps to get rid of your emotional wreckage and any debris you have from your past. It helps to protect your soul.

Obsidian is known for its grounding and stabilizing abilities, which makes it a great option for reigning in your scattered energy. If you start to feel as if you are being spread too thin, grab an obsidian and feel it restore all of your harmony and bring you back to Earth. Wearing jewelry with obsidian can leave you feeling renewed and confident.

When it comes to making layouts, obsidian can help to bring in a strong presence with its grounding abilities. If you feel as if you are lost in the clouds, it can cause unwelcome side effects, which can cause feelings of isolation and procrastination. If you are feeling spiritually lost, obsidian is able to bring you harmonious balance. Obsidian helps keep you anchored to Earth.

Lapis Lazuli

Since it was discovered, lapis lazuli has been one of the most sought after crystals. Its coloring is a celestial blue, which shows honor and royalty, vision and spirit, and Gods and power. This stone has always been a symbol of truth and wisdom.

During ancient times, they would use lapis lazuli to make a very valuable ultramarine dye. In Latin, lapis means "stone," and is Persian Lazhuward; it means "blue." This crystal is made up of many different minerals that include pyrite, calcite, sodalite, and lazurite.

Lapis lazuli is a great stone for psychologists, journalists, and executives. It is able to stimulate good judgment and wisdom. It will also help historians and archeologists with their intellectual analysis. It can help lawyers to solve problems. It is also able to provide writers and inventors with new and creative ideas.

It can help to stimulate the desire for knowledge, understanding, and truth. It is also able to help with the learning process, and can improve your memory. It is considered a stone of truth, and can help to encourage honesty of the written and spoken word, and spirit.

Labradorite

This stone can help you to find the magic within your spirit and to connect to the Universe. It is one of the best stones to help fight off a philosophical crisis. It is a shimmering, mythical light that separates the normal world from unseen realms. It is a magic stone. A crystal of healers, diviners, shamans, and anyone who travels and embraces the universe while seeking guidance and knowledge. It is great to help you awaken your psychic abilities, intuition, and being aware of your inner spirit. The labradorite reminds us to keep life magical by helping us link ourselves to the spiritual world where anything is possible.

Labradorite is considered a protector. It helps to shield your aura and to strengthen your natural energy. It will also help to protect you against misfortunes, negativity, and provides you with a safe exploration into the alternate levels of your consciousness.

You can expand your spiritual awareness by accessing the labradorite's magic. Hold a labradorite stone in each hand. You will soon feel your consciousness begin to expand. You can place a piece of smoky quartz between your feet to keep you grounded.

If you want to become more spiritual, grab a labradorite, and reach for the stars. It will seem like just another day in the neighborhood, but a labradorite will bridge the gap between Earth and Heaven. The Labradorite is associated with shamanism is an ancient form of spirituality where you can heal oneself in a different state of consciousness in a parallel plane of existence.

To quote Johann Wolfgang von Goethe: "Magic is believing in yourself. If you can do that, you can make anything happen. Basically, is it more than "pulling a rabbit out of a hat." It is more about finding your purpose in life, which will give you a sense of meaning and will make everything more lit up in your world.

Selenite

This is one of the most important crystals to have. It has also been known as "Satin Spar" because it has a milky shine that shines from its surface. Selenite is not known for its strength, but it can help to lighten the home's décor.

It gets its name from Selene, the Greek Goddess of the Moon. Before being polished, the stone can be recognized by its fibrous striations that run the length of the stone. While selenite isn't all that strong, it has a lot of power. The healing abilities of this stone focus on reaching higher planes and activation. It helps to connect to the third eye and crown chakra.

Selenite is also a cleansing stone and does not need to be cleansed like others. In fact, you can place other crystals on or near selenite to help cleanse and recharge them. A wand made of selenite can be used to cleanse your body as well as other stones.

Chapter 12: Picking Out Gems

If you have ever gone crystal shopping, you may have believed that you simply picked out your crystal based on how it looks or its color, but odds are, you picked it out because your intuition guided you to it, even if you didn't realize it. But sometimes crystal shopping isn't that easy. You may find that there are a bunch of different options, or other people start trying to recommend things. It could also be that you don't quite trust yourself. Picking out crystals aren't as simple as just grabbing one up. You need to make sure that you choose the stone that is meant for, and that's what we are going to go over now. Let's take a look at the different things that you can take into consideration when you are picking out your crystals.

1. What are their properties?

If you have a specific purpose for your crystal, then you can find your crystal a bit faster because you can search for them on websites or in books. Most books that are solely about crystals and their properties will have an index in the back sorted by the properties and not just by their name. Crystals can also be picked out based on their chakra associations.

Once you have narrowed down the crystals based on their properties and associations, you are still probably going to be left with quite a few options. That means you are going to have to tap into your intuition to narrow things down. If that doesn't work for you, don't worry, there are other steps.

2. What is your intuition telling you?

This means that you pick a crystal based on which one you are drawn to. You can feel drawn to crystals in person at a shop or through the photos you see online. Typically, seeing crystals in person will give you a stronger pull because you pick out the exact one you want of those that are in stock. Online, you can only be pulled to a certain type of crystal and not an exact one. You should always go with your initial feelings.

There are some crystals that will simply catch your eye. Continue to look through other options, and then go back to those that you liked the looks of and see how you feel. If you can, pick the crystal up. Does it want to remain in your hand? If so, then that is a good sign.

If you are looking at photos, try to figure out how the image makes you feel. Do you notice if you feel pulled toward that crystal? Does it make you feel excited? Instead of buying it right away, come back to it the next day, and if you feel the same way, then buy it. It is always interesting to me to look up the properties of a crystal that I have been drawn to buy afterward to see how accurate it was for my needs. This can actually be quite spooky.

3. Do you know how to dowse?

This is an advanced method of picking out crystals, and unless you already know how to dowse, you probably shouldn't do it. Dowsing involves holding onto a pendulum and asking it if a certain crystal would be right for you. If the pendulum gives you an yes, then you should get that crystal. You can do this to work through several different types of crystals, or you can also create a crystal dowsing chart.

4. Was the crystal given to you?

If you are ever given a crystal as a gift, then that crystal has found you. You will probably realize that the more you work with crystals, the more they will start to find you. It is also really common to end up losing your crystal, and while this can be upsetting, it typically means that the crystal has done all that it needs to do for you.

Buying Online

Being able to buy crystals online is a great convenience because you don't have to leave the house to do it, and it is really helpful if you don't have a metaphysical shop nearby. The main issue with this is that you can't touch them to really ready their vibrations.

Online buying will require you to use your intuition just a bit more. Browse through the various pictures and take note of what appeals to you the most. You may notice that you feel excited by a certain picture of crystal and that you feel a powerful need to touch it, and you feel frustrated because you are unable to do so. If you feel that you really want to be able to hold and touch that crystal and for it to become a part of your life, it is likely that you should buy it.

What if Nothing Calls to Me?

You shouldn't get discouraged if nothing calls to you. As with buying anything for a spiritual purpose, the intent is very important, and you might have to just face the fact that the timing is not right. If you aren't finding anything that stringing appeals to you at that moment in time, accept that this may not be the best time for you to purchase the crystal. You should then come back at another time, and then you may find that the same crystals you saw before jumps out at you and wants to be bought. Beware of buying crystals simply because you want to because you may end up with a collection of crystals that aren't going to help you with anything.

The last thing I can say about picking out crystals is that you should always expect the unexpected. You may set out to buy a certain type of crystal only to end up purchasing something that is completely different. You need to make sure that you are prepared to have your unconscious taken over. The unconscious tends to remain quiet in your regular life, so it does a great job when it comes to getting down to business and picking out the perfect crystal.

Chapter 13: Taking Care of Your Gems

Once you have picked our your crystals, the next thing you need to do is make sure you take care of your crystals. Crystals are like any other magical or spiritual tool you use. Before you ever use them, you should make sure that they have been charged and cleansed. Crystals are very sensitive to energies and will take in and amplify all energies around them.

You need to make sure you are careful when cleansing your crystals. You need to make sure you know if your crystals are heat or water sensitive. For example, selenite, halite, and azurite are all water soluble. Some crystals are porous, like turquoise, lapis lazuli, and opal. Pink quartz and amethysts can fade if they are left in direct sunlight for too long. If you aren't sure, a safe bet would be to place them outside under the light of a Full Moon. Moonlight isn't going to hurt your crystals and is a great way to cleanse them.

If you have people over and they end up touching your crystals without your permission, you will want to cleanse them once they leave. Trust me; you don't ever want to work with crystals that have been touched by other people. Their energy can end up hurting your work. The best way to make sure this doesn't happen is to keep your crystals somewhere others can't find them.

The cleansing rituals we are going to go over are able to be done at any time you feel your crystals need a cleansing. You should listen to your intuition when dealing with your crystals. If they don't feel right, then you should cleanse them. It isn't going to hurt them.

Sometimes people will say you should cleanse your crystals during a New Moon or waning moon, but if you know they have absorbed negativity, you should not wait. You shouldn't let negativity hang around for any longer than it has to.

These cleansing rituals are very simple. Before doing these, you can cast a circle, but you don't have to. Beginners tend to do better if they are working in a circle so that the energy is contained. None of these require an incantation, but if you feel like you need to say something, then follow your intuition.

Air Cleansing

Cleanings crystals with smoke is one of the oldest methods of cleansing. To do this cleansing, you are going to need incense or a smudge stick. The best options are copal, sage, or rosemary. Begin by lighting your incense and then pass your crystal through the smoke. As you do this, start to picture all of the impurities and negativities inside of them start to be burned away. This can be done as many times as you feel you need to. Let the incense burn out completely, or you can stub the smudge stick out in the Earth.

Earth Cleansing

This is the easiest cleansing method. With this cleansing, you are giving the energies back to the Earth. It works best when this is done outside. If you do this inside, you should use a bowl of salt, dirt, or sand. First, you will dig a hole and put your crystal inside of it. You should make sure that your crystal isn't going to dissolve while in the dirt, because some will. Let the crystal stay there and picture the Earth receiving all of the unwanted energies within your crystal. Leave the crystal is the Earth for as long as you feel like you need to.

Fire Cleansing

This is considered an aggressive but powerful cleansing method. Be careful not to burn yourself or your crystal. You will need a red candle for this. A fireplace will also work if you have one.

Light the candle and state your intent of cleansing your crystal and summon Fire into your space. Next, quickly pass your crystal through the flame and imagine that the fire is burning away all of its impurities and negativities. Do this for as long as you feel you need to. After you are done, let the candle burn out.

Water Cleansing

Water has long been viewed as a purifier. Any can of water can be used, and some people will even use oil. It is okay to use tap water, but if you are on city water and not well water, you may want to find water that is more pure.

There are two ways to do this. You can either plunge the whole crystal into the water, or simply drop a few drops on it if it is on the fragile side. After you do this, take some time to picture all of its bad energies being washed away. Let the crystal dry and get rid of the water you used.

Singing Bowl Cleansing

This is a fun way to cleanse crystals, even though singing bowls do tend to be on the expensive side. You can also use YouTube videos to get the same effect. Using your own singing bowl, if you can, place the crystal inside of the bowl. If it won't fit in the bowl, simply place it on the altar and sit the singing bowl on top of it so that it will be touch by its vibrations. Now is the time to play your singing bowl. As you hear the sounds echoing, really feel its vibrations. Allow the sounds to capture all of the unwanted energies within the item. Once the sound fades away, all of the bad energies will disappear with it.

Personal Energy Cleansing

You don't have to have anything special to cleanse your crystals with. Your mind is a great tool. This is a little more advanced, so beginners may have a hard time with it. In order for this to work, you need to be able to feel and use the energetic fields. If you aren't sure how to do this, then you need to start out practicing alone before you try to purify your crystals. Once you are ready to move up to your crystals, here's how:

First, picture a ray of light emanating for your hands. Take some time to really feel this light. Next, place both of your hands over the stone and picture that all of the unwanted energies are little black bubbles. The light coming from your hands is an energetic vacuum and is sucking up all of those energy remnants. Once everything is sucked up in your hands, picture all of the energy falling to the ground. To help you do this, you can touch the floor with your hands. This is very important because you want to get rid of all of that energy. Push it all back into the Earth.

Connecting To Your Crystals

Once your crystals are cleansed, you will need to take a bit of time to connect with them. The best way to do this is to meditate with your crystal to help connect you with its energy. This will help them to work more efficiently, and it will help to improve your psychic abilities. It's also relaxing.

Take the crystal in your non-dominant hand. Get into a comfortable position and then gaze upon your crystal for a few minutes. Look at all of the little details in the crystal until you can accurately picture it in your mind. Close your eyes. Now, focus on the sensation of your crystal. Tap into all of your senses to really feel the crystal. Now, take it beyond your physical senses and see if you can feel its vibrations. This will be a personal experience and will be different for every crystal you do this with. Once you feel you have been in meditation for long enough, you can open your eyes and move into programming your crystal.

Programming Crystals

The next part is the fun part. This is a lot like consecrating a tool. You are infusing the crystal with your intention. You will need to have a specific goal in mind to do this. But, you don't have to program your crystals in order to use them. If the crystal is not programmed, you can still use its inherent properties, but it won't be as focused. Again, the important this is to pay attention to your intuition. You are going to know whether or not you should program the crystal.

All you have to have to program your crystal is to focus on an intention. It is best if the intention corresponds with the properties of the crystal. Once you have your intention, you can meditate with the crystal again and fill it with your intention. You can also just "ask" your crystal to help you with your intention. You can also visualize the words being writing into the crystal. You can even use and oil and draw a sigil of your intention on the crystal. There are endless possibilities.

That's about it when it comes to caring for your crystals. The most important thing to find out, though, is to find out how your crystals will take to salt, water, and heat. Some crystals don't care, and you cleanse them; however you want. Then there are some crystals that don't like certain things. The last thing you want to do is to destroy the crystals you just picked out, so do a little research before cleansing it.

Chapter 14: Crystal Spells

In this final chapter, we are going to go over different spells that you can do that places crystals at the forefront. One last thing before we get into the spells is that you should never do a spell simply because it sounds interesting. You should always have an intention that you are working towards before you pick a spell. You'll also find that many of the spells will use candles as well as herbs.

Give of Drinking/Smoking Spell

You are going to need:

- Amethyst

- Glass of water

- Black string

- An empty alcohol bottle that has been washed and has a lid

- A pen

- 10 to 15 small paper pieces

Take a bit of time before you start to think about why you want to give up alcohol. If you have an actual physical addiction, you should speak with your doctor first because quitting cold turkey can endanger your health.

Now, write down all of the reasons for stopping drinking on each slip of the paper.

Now, cast your circle and take a few moments to meditate until you feel calm and clear-minded. Pick up a piece of paper and read it. Then, you need to affirm the opposite of that, as if you have stopped drinking. Then bask in how this would feel if it were true right now. Picture yourself as being a non-drinker and rejoice in a healthy and happy feeling. Place the paper into the bottle. Continue to do this until you have gone through every piece of paper. Next, tie the black cord around the neck of the bottle and tie three knots.

Pick up the water and picture white light coming out of it. Slowly drink that water, and feel all of that light pouring into you with every sip. Feel it bless and purify you.

Pick up the amethyst and cup it in your hands. Feel all of this white light spinning through your body. Feel it becoming stronger and then feel it flow into that amethyst. Picture the crystal pulsing with the energy. Sit in meditation for a little bit, until you know that you are done.

Say: "I am a non-drinker. So mote it be."

Feel that this is a true statement. You can now close your circle. You can dispose of the bottle either by burying it or throwing it out. Carry the amethyst with you. If you feel like you need to drink, have a glass of water instead.

If you want to stop smoking, all you have to write down the reasons for giving up smoking, and change the incantation to "I am a non-smoker. So mote it be."

A Crystal Love Spell

You are going to need:

- Pink yarn

- Red cloth

- Rose quartz

- Moonstone

- Two apple seeds

- Ground cinnamon

- Dried basil

- Pink candle

- Red candle

This spell is best done during the Full Moon.

Before you begin, make sure you take a moment to clarify what type of relationship you are looking to have. Make sure that you are clear on what your desire is. This can take some time. It is also a good idea to figure out how you feel about it and not allow yourself to get hung up on the details. For example, instead of listing out all of the traits you want them to have, write down that you want to be attracted to them. Also, think about how you want to feel in the relationship.

Get your items together and then cast your circle. Light the candles and spread the red cloth out in front of you. Pass the moonstone through the flames of the candles and then sit it on the cloth. Repeat this for the rose quartz.

Pick up the apple seeds, and say: "By the light of the moon, I now plant these seeds of love."

As you sit these seeds onto the cloth along with the crystals, start seeing all of the soft pink energy coming from the crystals and nourishing your seeds with their loving energy. Sprinkle everything with some cinnamon and basil. Pull the four corners of the cloth together so that everything is wrapped inside, and then wrap the pink yarn around the bag three times. Tie the bag with three knots and say: "So mote it be."

You can close out your circle and then keep the bag you just made with you to attract love.

Increase Confidence Spell

You are going to need:

- Clothes in orange, red, or yellow – optional

- Solar anointing oil

- Tiger's eye crystal

- Yellow or gold candle

Place all of your tools in the middle of what will become your circle. Start by meditating on what you would like the spell to do for you. Make sure that you are crystal clear about what you want the outcome to be, such as, what areas of your life do you need more confidence? How would you want to act in different situations? Specifics will improve this spell.

Now, you can cast your circle and then sit in the middle of it so that you are facing south. Pick up the candle and anoint it with the solar oil as you say: "I call upon the energies of the Sun and Earth to help me find my confidence and worth."

Now, light your candle and set it in front of you. Pick up the tiger's eye and let your hand cup around it. Gaze at the flame and picture a golden light shining over you. Have this light become vibrant and beautiful. This is all of the unconditional love that the Universe has for you. As you allow this golden

144

energy to wash over you, see yourself in the eyes of the God and Goddess. See them loving you like a parent would their child. They love you simply because you exist. There are no conditions attached to that love. Feel your heart expanding with this energy. Watch as the light continues to grow bigger. It starts to fill the circle and then spills out into the entire room. Take as much time as you need to in order to visualize this.

After you feel that the room is completely filled with this light, open up your hands and begin to feel the tiger's eye taking in all of this energy. Watch as the golden light pours into the crystal until it is all held within it.

After you are finished, close your circle and carry your tiger's eye with you and use all of its energy whenever you need some unconditional love by holding it and meditating for a moment.

A Charm Bottle for Friendship

This spell is best done on a Friday during the Full or waxing Moon, but if you can't align it just so, it will still work.

You are going to need:

- Pink, brown, or yellow candle

- Three drops of lemon juice

- Three sun-dried lemon slices

- Three lemon seeds

- Six coriander seeds – or other friendship herbs

- Tiger's eye

- Pentacle plate – optional

- Cauldron – optional

- Scissors

- Black pen

- Yellow paper

- Glass jar with lid

- Palo Santo or Sage

Start by cleansing yourself with the Palo Santo or sage and then cast your circle in your favorite way. Using the same smudge, cleanse all of the items that you are going to be using in your spell. Picture all of the items being surrounded by a yellow light and know that every one of the items will bring new friends into your life.

Sit the jar onto the pentacle plate or your altar if you aren't using the plate. Picture that as you fill it with items, that your life is also being filled with new friends. Imagine yourself as being happy.

Cut the sheet of yellow paper into strips, and one each of the strips write one quality or trait that you would like your new friends to have. While you write these things down, say these things out loud, and picture the friend that you are creating with these qualities. It is very important that you never, ever, write down a specific person. You are trying to bring the person to you that will be the best fit for you, and it may not be the one you believe is the best for you.

One at a time, pick the strips of paper up, say the trait, picture the friend, light it on fire, and let it burn away into your cauldron. Continue to picture the person as the strip of paper burns. Then place the ashes inside of the jar. Continue with all of the strips. If you do not have a cauldron or heat-proof bowl, you can simply fold the piece of paper and then unfold to release its magic and place it inside of the jar. If you are using the folded paper method, one fold is for a single friend being called into your life; multiple folds will bring more than one friend.

Now, add in the lemon seeds, one by one, while you say: "Into this jar, I drop this seed to manifest into my need. I wish that my number of friends will grow, based on the qualities I've place below. So mot it be."

Place the tiger's eye stone into the jar and say: "Tiger's eye to keep away false friends, and allow me to see the friends who will be loyal until the end. So mote it be."

Add the coriander and say: "Coriander to invoke Universal love, a love that has been absent from my life. So mote it be."

Place in the lemon slices and say: "A lemon slice, the color yellow, place into this bottle to show just how much the fruit called our friendship will grow. So mote it be."

Next, add in the lemon juice and say: "Lemon juice, meant to preserve, serve the purpose you were meant to serve. Preserve this friendship, every little drop, let us remain good friends until time stops. So mote it be."

Finish off the spell by place the lid onto the jar and seal it with some wax from the candle. Take a moment to visualize the amazing friendship you have just created as you see a pink or yellow light surrounding the bottle. Close your circle and thank anybody you have called in and know that the spell is complete.

A Spell for Glamour

You are going to need:

- Makeup or jewelry you want to wear

- Cotton ball or pad

- Micellar water

- Rose quartz

- Red candle

- Palo Santo stick

- Small mirror

Start by lighting the Palo Santo and use it to cleanse your work space and all of the items that you are going to be using. Next, cast your circle in order to keep all of the energies housed into your sacred space.

Now decorate your sacred space with the mirror and any extra rose quartz that you may have. Place a rose quartz into your micellar way and then say: "Pasithea, Aphrodite, see my wishes shine through brightly."

Pick the mirror up in your non-dominant hand, left hand for right handed people, and vice versa. Now gaze upon the part of your face that you would like to change. Say: "My (state the part you want to change) seen only to me. I create the canvas for others to see."

As you are still looking at yourself, dip your piece of cotton into the micellar water. Say: "Now a canvas, I wipe it clean. Only what I visualize shall be seen."

Start wiping the potion over all of your face, making sure that you pay more attention to the part that you would like to change. As you are cleansing, let your vision go a bit blurry, like you do when you are crying.

Gaze into the mirror and see what you would like other people to see when they see you. Make sure that you can see all of your face intact as well. After you are satisfied with what you are visualizing, say: "What I see will be seen by all, until I let my glamour fall. And it harms none, so mote it be."

Lay your mirror down and thank Pasithea and Aphrodite and then close your circle.

This glamour will take several visualization processes, and it will take a lot of energy to keep up. Every time you look in the mirror, take a moment to visualize your glamour. Those who don't know you that well will notice your glamour first, and then with time, people who are close to will be able to see it as well. Eventually, it will become second nature.

A Spell for Friendship

You are going to need:

- Yellow or orange candle

- A teaspoon of dried allspice

- Carnelian

- Orange pouch

Before you start your spell, really take the time to figure out what kind of friendship you would like to bring into your life. Do you want a small group of close-knit friends, or a lot of friends? What about their personalities and hobbies? What kind of qualities or values do they need?

Take as long as you need to on this step so that you get the friends that you want.

Next, cleanse all of the objects that you are using. This could be through visualization or smudging. Start by casting your circle and doing any prep work that you need to like meditating or calling your spirit guides.

Then, light the candle. Sit everything else out in front of you. Place the carnelian in the middle of your pouch and make a circle of allspice around it.

Shut your eyes for a moment and picture yourself surrounded by all of your friends. These are all positive people that you like to be with. Make this come to life in your mind's eye and really focus on the positive feelings that your friendship brings. Once you have these strong feelings, place your hands, palms down, over the spices, and crystals. Picture these feelings like a gold light moving out of your heart, through your arms, and then down your palms, filling the objects with the light. Picture your objects soaking up all of this golden light until they are pulsating with its energy.

Put everything inside of the pouch and close it. Pick up the candle and draw three circles above the pouch in a clockwise direction as you say: "True friendships, come to me, as I will, so mote it be."

Thank everything you called into your spell and close your circle.

Carry this pouch with you where ever you go to attract the friends you want into your life.

Spell for Self-Empowerment

You are going to need:

- Citrine, rhodonite, amethyst, or rose quartz

- Yarrow

- Orange or lemon essential oil

- Light or matches

- Red candle

Begin by anointing the candle with your chosen essential oil and then sprinkle it with or roll it in the yarrow. Now, light the candle. Focus completely on the flame of the candle and on raising your energy.

Pick up the crystal and then wave it through the flame of the candle and then say: "I am love, I am power, I am enough, I am joy, I am good." Make sure that you will pop the word "am." Continue to chant this for as long as you are able to. Keep this chant in your mind every day to remind yourself of your personal power. Keep this crystal on you when you need extra confidence. You can also take a moment to visualize the flame of the candle and chant the mantra whenever you need to.

Charm Bag for Cleansing and Protection

You are going to need:

- Sage essential oil

- Candle holder

- Matches

- Black candle

- Lavender buds – optional

- Lavender essential oil

- Dried rose petals

- Dried thyme leaves

- Jet or black obsidian stone

- Dried sage leaves

- Piece of white or black ribbon

- Square of black fabric

Begin by casting your circle however; you choose to. Take a moment to clear and relax your mind. Next, anoint your candle with some of the sage oil, and then roll it in the thyme and sage leaves.

Light your candle and picture yourself feeling protects, cleansed, and pure. As the candle burns, let the smoke waft over the fabric, ribbon, and everything that will go in it. Do this and say the following three times:

"Cleanse my soul, I ask of thee, cleanse me of my negativity. Wishes and energy, thoughts and deeds, cleanse them all, so mote it be. As you cleanse, protect my soul to, through night and day, and the morning dew. Protect me from harm and negativity, cleanse it now, and leave only purity. It is done."

Once you have said this three times, and everything has been passed through the smoke, blow the candle out and then put everything in the middle of the piece of fabric and then draw up the edges and close it with the ribbon.

Do the same thing every day until the candle has completely burned out. Bury the leftover wax in the dirt. Keep your charm bag with you and repeat the candle process if you start feeling as if you need a boost.

Conclusion

Thank you for making it through to the end of *Wiccan Spells*, let's hope it was informative and able to provide you with all of the tools you need to achieve your goals whatever they may be.

The next step is to start to use what you have learned to improve your Wiccan practice. You can choose to focus only on Moon, crystal, or candle magic, or you can choose to incorporate all of them into your practice. As you probably have already realized, they all work together quite well. Very few Witches choose to use one or the other because they realize, when used together, it intensifies their power. Above all, make sure you work with what resonates with you. Don't do something simply because I said you could. Do things that feel right to you and your practice.

Finally, if you found this book useful in any way, a review on Amazon is always appreciated!

Printed in Great Britain
by Amazon

65901991R00095